Gravity Never Stops

Also by Ron Sieh
T'ai Chi Ch'uan: The Internal Tradition

Gravity Never Stops

The Life and Training of a Martial Artist

A

Ron Sieh

North Atlantic Books
Berkeley, California

Published by
North Atlantic Books
P.O. Box 12327
Berkeley, California 94712

Cover design by Julie Tilka
Text design by Brad Greene
Printed in the United States of America
Distributed to the book trade
by Publishers Group West

Gravity Never Stops: The Life and Training of a Martial Artist is sponsored by the Society for the Study of Native Arts and Sciences, a nonprofit educational corporation whose goals are to develop an educational and crosscultural perspective linking various scientific, social, and artistic fields; to nurture a holistic view of arts, sciences, humanities, and healing; and to publish and distribute literature on the relationship of mind, body, and nature.

North Atlantic Books' publications are available through most bookstores. For further information, call 800-337-2665 or visit our website at www.northatlanticbooks.com.

Substantial discounts on bulk quantities are available to corporations, professional associations, and other organizations. For details and discount information, contact our special sales department.

Library of Congress Cataloging-in-Publication Data

Sieh, Ron.
    Gravity never stops : the life and training of a martial artist / by Ron Sieh.
    p. cm.
    Summary: "Ron Sieh, a learned martial artist and teacher, offers a narrative that traces his life from adolescence to adulthood and the changes brought about by his study of internal martial arts"—Provided by publisher.
    ISBN 1-55643-502-9 (pbk.)
    1. Sieh, Ron. 2. Martial artists—United States—Biography. 3. Martial arts—United States. I. Title.
    GV1113.S55A3 2004
    796.8'092—dc22
                                                    2004021772

1 2 3 4 5 6 7 8 9 DATA 09 08 07 06 05 04

> **Contents** <

1

An Angry Young Man

I was once a very angry young man.

I was born in 1953 in Moline, Illinois. We moved to Bloomington, Minnesota when I was two.

All through my childhood I was small, skinny, lost, and confused. I thought I was ugly. My ears were way too big. The kids who picked on me called me several names, but the one that was most painful was "big ears." I didn't have buckteeth, but I did have a big overbite and kids latched onto that too. Being called "big ears" back then made me think something was wrong with me. That thought got a grasp on my sense of self, my confidence, my place in the world. I still have big ears, but my sense of self, my confidence, and my place in the world all have changed.

I despised my younger brother Rob—which was probably misplaced anger about my parents. Dad emotionally abandoned us. Mom went a bit crazy after the divorce. I had poor communication with adults. There was no adult to talk to, certainly no wise elder. In any case, my parents never imparted to me a sense of self-confidence. We did do some pretty interesting things, though, now that I think of it. Dad had these little go-carts called "quarter midgets," and my brother and I used to race them at a small permanent carnival called Queen Anne Kiddieland. It was a one-quarter mile dirt track frequently sprayed down with oil to reduce dust. And he built a helicopter-like device called a "gyro-copter" for his own private use. I remember going to airports with my dad to pull it up and down the runway with a car and a rope like a kite, and getting kicked out of them for taking up runway space. So we did stuff nobody in the neighborhood ever even considered doing. But as far as just getting down and playing with us like a normal dad, I don't recall any of that. Yet I did get tucked into bed every night with a kiss when I was young. And one of the things I also got from Dad is: if you do something, do it really well. Being good at something is cool. He'd take us to those "Spaghetti Westerns," and we'd learn from the Clint Eastwood character, if you're going to use a gun, use it right.

One other thing Dad and I had in common: learning to play the Hammond Spinnet organ. My dad was taking organ lessons, and one time he brought me with him to see his teacher in this dingy old five-story building in downtown Minneapolis. I started taking lessons too, but it wasn't something we really did together. Basically, what my parents had to do with it was that they made me practice. To get me to the lessons, they'd give me thirty-five cents, and I'd go to the corner and take the bus all the way to downtown Minneapolis, all by myself. Rather unheard of today. For a nine-year-old to do that. But I did it.

I started from nothing and got really good at it really fast. And I played all the pop classics. I played in concerts and I played in contests and I won trophies. But the truth is that I never really enjoyed it. I was learning under duress. I never learned the songs that I wanted to—no rock 'n' roll, nothing like that. I was made to practice my lesson and wasn't allowed to play anything more. Just my lesson. But I was good at my lesson and it became a kind of competitive thing. I was in competition with one of my dad's friends' children. Russ was the kid's name. And he practiced hours a day and worked really hard at it. I didn't. I practiced my half an hour a day. But when we actually competed against each other in contests, I won. So that was great for my self-esteem at a time when I really needed it. I played the organ until I was probably seventeen and then just stopped. I wasn't interested because even at that age I still had to play what my parents wanted me to play, so I quit. But knowing that I was good at it and that I had gained a skill at something like that was very important. I still think it was important. I knew in my bones that if you actually did practice something, you got better at it. That served me well when I took up martial arts.

❮

What was the neighborhood like where I grew up? It was white, middle-class—a typical "Readers Digest" world in a south suburb of Minneapolis. My parents bought their house there for $12,000. Today it's worth $150,000.

My parents' divorce happened when I was about thirteen years old and that really screwed up my Mom, though she did handle things pretty well considering. She didn't get any financial support from my dad, and she raised us three boys all by herself. She was kind of a hellion—she had no problem taking out the wooden spoon when things didn't go right—but as far as food and clothing and all of that was concerned, she was great.

❯

It was very hard to go to school. I hated it. I remember sitting in the classroom, being force-fed information, very little of which I was interested in. All I wanted to do was be outside in the woods. School was a crime.

I was a tender kid. I couldn't handle the way other kids treated me. I faked illnesses a lot. That was one of the ways I learned that I could actually make my body do things I wanted it to—like have an earache! Tragic, but I did. I got through school without any major calamities. I actually have very few memories of it.

I didn't play football or hockey. I played some baseball and was pretty good at it. I had natural talent but no encouragement; no one even took time to explain the rules or strategy. I worried more about making mistakes than enjoying the game.

I had one friend. Wayne. He was the other outcast. I didn't hang out with a gang of boys. Well, we did a bit. Playing army and that kind of stuff. But as far as individual friends were concerned, I only had Wayne—another misfit.

By the time I was in high school, I had a lot in common with the Columbine shooters of a few years ago. I felt victimized. I had access to guns. I owned a .22. But I wasn't living in a culture that showed hundreds of killings a week on TV and at the cinema. I wasn't saturated with violence and murderous imagery. We lived in Readers Digest Land, like I said. The best things on TV were Walt Disney's "Wonderful World of Color," "Lost in Space," and "Sea Hunt." No murders every night, no bloody stuff or titilating sex. *Pong* was the hot video game. Killing another human being was a very, very big deal. You really had to be messed up to kill somebody. Most kids were afraid enough of adults, so they generally did what they were told. There was even—get this—spanking in schools!

The political atmosphere of my Readers' Digest home-town was typical of the U.S. in the '50s. We thought our government had integrity, that the guys in charge had our own best interests on the front burner, that the bad guys were all in Russia and China, that American work-ers were noble. Of course, I'm not suggesting that this is the way it was, but it was how it was perceived by the people I knew growing up in Middle America.

Mine was a time of Andy Griffith, Lassie, Marcus Welby, M.D.—all pretty wholesome fare. Good and evil were clear. Gangsters didn't kill innocents; the bad guys would be brought to justice. I knew what a family was. It was two parents, one female and one male, brothers and/or sisters, and a house. Men were men; women were women. Very simplistic and clear. Rigid roles of behav-ior defined manliness and womanliness. It was a time of very little exploration of roles or consciousness. In many ways it was stifling and critical; yet, on the other side of the coin, people generally knew how to act.

For most of us in my generation what we did with our *attention* wasn't even a consideration. It was some-thing we took for granted, like breathing or being "alive." The idea of *training* attention, of studying "being," was utterly foreign. It probably would have been considered a Communist plot back then—or a José Jimenez com-edy routine. Popeye spoke for us all: "I am what I am what I am." Anyone who questioned that was a freak or a faggot. And yet a counterculture was developing all around us.

I used to read comics a lot. I was really interested in the Karate Kid (the original Karate kid, not Ralph Macchio). He was a DC Comics superhero. He took on Superboy and Chameleon and Kid Flash and all those. He wanted to join with the others but he had a lot of doubts because he was just an ordinary guy. DC Comics had something called "The Justice League of America." When the Kid wanted to join the league, the other superheroes wouldn't let him in because he was just an ordinary human being who didn't have any special powers. But he did know Ju Jitsu and Judo and Karate. To prove himself he took on Superboy. Now Superboy, of course, had an unfair advantage: he had that red cape. Superboy ended up beating the Karate Kid, but for the first few seconds the Karate Kid, a mere mortal, was winning, throwing Superboy around. So the other superheroes let him in. Karate Kid was my hero—just a regular guy who was trying to join the club. The notion of attaining great skill and agility without possessing super powers—that became my goal in life.

Karate Kid didn't have a comic of his own, he was just a character in *Superboy,* but this was pretty much the first exposure I had to martial arts. I don't think I ever saw a Bruce Lee movie as a kid.

I remember puffing myself up in Cub Scouts and

telling people that I knew Karate, and getting in trouble for it—a gang of kids at a Cub Scout group at church were waiting for me to the leave the building to beat me up because I bragged that I knew Karate. And I didn't. I knew nothing. I called my Mom, and she came and rescued me.

I was only in one real fight in school. I was picked on throughout my childhood, but one day in the ninth grade I got into an actual fight. In my high school there was a hierarchy. Everybody knew who could beat up whom. One day the friend of "Number One" started to pick on me, and I fought him and I won. Neither of us really got hurt. In fact, we got pulled apart. But I hit him a couple of times and there was blood, and he didn't hit me. All of a sudden I was really somebody. The next day, when I walked down the hall, everybody parted the way—it was like the Red Sea! So I discovered the thrill of combat! What you can get out of it. It was an important experience. It gave me a lot of confidence. After that, I didn't get into a lot of fights, but I wasn't running away from them either. One day something happened, and I pushed a kid up against a wall, and that greatly enhanced my reputation. Sad.

One of the ways boys had of greeting each other was with a punch—you punch somebody in the arm, and then the guy who got punched would punch you back, and that would go back and forth, and whoever would hit the hardest and last the longest, that person would win. And that's how you'd greet each other. A terrible way to greet each other. But we did that.

In high school, there was always an aura of danger. Of course it wasn't anything like the real danger that there is today—there wasn't anything like crack, or knives, or guns—just a sense of always testing who was the toughest.

❤

Everything decidedly changed for me when I got into meditation in the Army. I'll get back to this in a minute. I was nineteen years old. I joined the military right out of high school. I was lost at the time, didn't know what to do, and was just hanging out. We didn't know what slackers were back then, but we were doing a fairly prophetic imitation. Then one day my best friend suddenly said, "I'm gonna join the Army," and I thought, "Why not? Let's check it out. Jeez, what's happening with the Vietnam War these days?" It was *Apocalypse Now* time, 1971, and the draft had just ended. We knew we had cleared the window to go to Vietnam.

I started off in Missouri doing basic training, eight weeks of drills. It was overwhelming. The routine hit me so hard I had no time to feel much of anything. I wasn't homesick until I went home on leave for a week before getting reassigned.

Basic training was a real wake-up call. I remember running and passing people throwing up, and the drill sergeant saying if you drop out you've got to run another five miles. Basic training was different then than it is today. It was my first initiation from boyhood to manhood. When I came home, my mother gave me cigarette. I was supposed to be a man! And in retrospect, well, I could do a lot of pushups, and I had this green uniform, and people called me an army man at the airport, but was this manhood? I don't think so.

During basic training, there was a group of people doing Karate-Do on base, so I joined the class. It wasn't part of our regular training. In fact, the regular training in the Army may have looked real good, but it was just enough to get you killed!

This Karate-Do class was put together after the day's training in a space rented by a couple of Army black belts. One guy did Tae-Kwon-Do; the other did Karate-Do. Because of that, there was lots of back-and-forth competition.

Right after basic training, everybody took a test to see where their interests lay. A guy I had never met before and never saw again afterwards came up to me, started talking, and asked if I wanted to be in the infantry. I said, "No way. Absolutely not!"

He was ready for that: "Well, any questions that have to do with the outdoors, hiking, camping?" Answer: "No,

I hate it, never did it." That pretty much kept me out of the infantry. Because I knew math from school, I got involved in artillery. After basic training, I got sent to "beautiful" Oklahoma—Fort Still, outside of Lawton; that's the field-artillery capital of America. I became an instructor, teaching people how to put a Pershing nuclear missile together. Our rocket rode on a tractor-trailer; it had to be kept moving so that the Russians couldn't target them all. Kind of scary—that we were the ones in charge of the weapons of the Four Horsemen, assembling and disassembling them. What did we know about anything?

But it was fun, too. We were a brotherhood of boys moving into men. We had major stuff in common. We all hated the military. We all complained together. There was this joke going around: "What's the difference between the Boy Scouts and the military? Well, the Boy Scouts have adult leadership."

At Fort Still there were two systems of martial arts, as I mentioned. There was a black belt from one system, and then there was another black belt from another system. There was a fierce competition between brands of martial arts. They would contradict each other and get in fights. It lasted about six months and then it kind of fell apart.

When I first got to Fort Still, I met a guy from Louisiana who boxed, so I boxed with him for a while, maybe my first year there. From the beginning of my training in martial arts, I was interested in actual combat. I wanted to learn how to fight better. Even later, when I was studying things like T'ai Chi, which are often taught without the fighting component, I was still interested in it in order to learn how to fight better.

▲

The army wasn't all learning to fight and assemble missiles. It was an exposure to all sorts of things that we never heard of back in Minnesota. I had always been kind of a weird kid, but in Minnesota I had no opportunity to explore much "countercultural" stuff. I knew it was there, but I never saw it in Bloomington. Before I enlisted in the Army, I had been up to Canada a couple of times fishing, and I had visited my grandparents in Illinois. That's about it. It wasn't until the Army that I heard *Led Zeppelin* for the first time or was exposed to people from different parts of the country.

Back in the '70s, the Army was a drugstore. People did a lot of drugs. LSD and pot were mine. In those days, everything was love, peace, *Crosby, Stills, Nash, and Young.* Very different from today.

One night at Fort Still, I was in the back seat of a car with an Army buddy, tripping on LSD, and I saw the book *Be Here Now* by Richard Alpert. I thought, "What is this!?" My buddy said it was cool; he really liked the cover; his interest didn't go much beyond that. The cover *was* great—this geometric shape that said, "Be Here Now! Be Here Now! Be Here Now!" on the top, the bottom, upside-down, and on the left side and the right side.

I read *Be Here Now*—and I read it in the right context and at the right moment. I was this little white boy from the suburbs in the army, right out of basic training. When I got to Fort Still, the first thing I found there was LSD. And *Be Here Now*. I read it cover to cover. I must have been ripe, because the next day I was a vegetarian and doing the yoga in the back of the book. And I kept doing it every day.

The jacket of *Be Here Now* didn't say it in so many words, but the book was put together for people in my situation—tripping. It was all about Alpert (who's now called Ram Dass) and Timothy Leary—their experiences with LSD and Alpert finding a guru. I took my buddy's copy and read the book in one sitting. In the Army being vegetarian meant eating only desserts and maybe potatoes sometimes even though they had saltpeter on them.

After *Be Here Now,* I started reading Buddhist stuff. One book that I remember from around that time (I was in the army from 1971 to 1973) was *Cutting Through Spiritual Materialism* by Chogyam Trungpa. Great book. It really influenced the way I write. I love Chogyam Trungpa, though I never actually studied with him.

Another book I read at Fort Still was *Bury My Heart*

at Wounded Knee. I was learning for the first time about the unbelievable atrocities against Indians—and there I was—a part of the Army—the bad guys—and at Fort Still, which is where they sent their Indian prisoners.

Meanwhile, Fort Still itself was a kind of trip. Since it was a field-artillery base, every month they had a firepower demonstration where they'd blow off several million dollars worth of stuff. Huey helicopters would come with mini-guns and blast balloons attached to the ground—hundreds and hundreds of them, just disappearing under thousands of rounds a minute from the air. You'd also see brass casings falling from the helicopters like rain. Artillery from miles in back of us would fire over our heads at boulders painted white—poof! poof!—while phantom jets zoomed low in the sky.

There was also the Honest John missile—it's very obsolete now; it was a one-piece rocket on a tractor-trailer. It erected to the perfect "erection angle" and went off. (I won't tell you the jokes about that.) By the time the Honest John rocket leaves its twenty-foot rail, it's moving at the speed of sound. Lots of flames. Very impressive. Then it explodes on the other side of the horizon, making a fake mushroom cloud. Everybody would be stoned and clapping. It was like a rock concert—very dramatic, great special effects, and very expensive.

2

Being Alive

My two years in the army introduced me to a cultural attitude and encouraged me to adopt it. But the influence of my reading and my first exposure to the martial arts introduced me to the idea of being really alive.

Being alive is a thing all by itself. It came first, before schools, before television, and before any of the rules and goals of civilization. The challenge of being alive can't be changed by any of those things. If you want to fight the rules, fight the schools, go ahead. But don't fight being alive. That's our gift from the Great Mystery. A lifetime is our opportunity to realize human potential.

Most of us are not farmers or gardeners or any of those occupations that work with the natural environment. Most of us toil indoors on a computer or in a factory doing work that has little to do with our lives beyond bringing home a paycheck. We have virtual lives in a virtual world in which the spiritually nourishing and healing natural world has been quantified and given a price tag. Have we gotten so far away from what our lives really are that we laugh at the idea of belonging to something wholesome, genuine, and true?

Inner exploration is not supported by the common culture. Everything we are taught about how to be in the world is outwardly motivated. The notion of personal liberation as freedom from the bonds of suffering is supplanted by making money, lifestyle, guarding privacy, collecting SUVs or snowmobiles.

Where is the magic? What do those people who live in the rain forests find so great about it? What does being born and dying in the wild, part of the web of life and death, offer that having a good job and making a lot of money (so that you can vacation and see the rainforest) doesn't? What is your life like in a world of concrete and arcades and constant stress?

There's a rap song called, "You're Nobody Till Somebody Kills You." Very cute. In some circles, a virgin is a person who has never killed anyone, not someone who hasn't had sex.

Some gang cultures make you put your life on the line at incredible odds (against you) for things that just aren't worth it. Then you're dead; you've made it. Unfortunately you've blown your gift.

You better make sure that what you're getting is worth the price. I'm not saying some things aren't. Just make sure.

They won't tell you, though. Not the schools, not the

gangs, not the television or the Internet, not even your buddies. You've got to find that out for yourself, inside yourself. Otherwise, you've fallen for the Great Scam instead of the Great Mystery—and paid, like they say, "the ultimate price."

Youth culture, when I was growing up, was a culture of anger. It still is today.

What were we so angry about? Why were we so pissed off? What were we pissed off at?

That everyone's out for themselves, that it's the law of the jungle out there;

That the world's poisoned, and no one really gives a shit about cleaning up air and water if there's money to be made polluting;

That your supposed elders mouth off about clean air, clean water—but you know, and I know, and even they know they're not going to do anything about it except maybe make rules that can't be enforced;

That all government is one step removed from the mafia, serving corporate godfathers;

That the politicians try out different lies to see which sound best;

That schools are bureaucracies set up to benefit drones and serve community fascists;

That ancient warrior cultures are killed off like weeds;

That appearances rule—money, looks, fists, cheap smiles, guns, basketball shoes, jewelry.

And it's not just North America. If you're born in the wrong part of Sierra Leone, a guy might chop off your arm or hand just for walking in the wrong place or having the wrong look on your mug. If you plead with him, get down on your knees and beg, tell him that he is taking away your livelihood and all your hope, he might just laugh and chop off both hands instead of one, to make his point. That's the kind of world we've made this. If you're born in parts of Southeast Asia, your parents might sell you to a brothel in Bangkok or Kosovo, or you might be kidnapped and sold into slavery in Saudi Arabia.

That a business will destroy a sustainable and beneficial rival to increase its own profit;

That America's treaties with the natives mean nothing—or turn into casinos.

Who'd want to be here? If this is what life is, I might as well be dead, or get killed trying.

I once asked an angry high-school girl what she was so pissed off about. "Everything," she said. "Everything your generation has done to the world."

"How do you want to fix it?"

"I don't want to fix it. I want to destroy it."

I can understand this sort of anger. I was born into the same polluted world, where money rules, where who we are supposed to be and what we are supposed to think is small, shallow, and safe.

My parents wanted me to sign on, get a job, get married, have kids, and stop growing. Safety first! They were uninterested in anything grand, exploratory, exalted. The vision I inherited was tiny and lame, and then I waited twenty-five years for the Revolution that never came.

Our natural impulse to explore our depths and capabilities as humans is directed towards getting good job, and afterwards retirement. Spending money is what interests us.

Just think of it: we're given *lives* and no one is taught what such things *are* or how to use them. All the old meanings are up for grabs. No wonder some kids just think of shooting their rivals and tormentors and then turning the artillery on themselves. If you don't know what a life really is, if you don't feel it, if you don't feel yourselves in this world, then how can you tell what anything is or what it's worth? How can you know the consequences of an act if the act has no reality?

Everything is made to seem like a game, played for a round—cut and roll again, like in a movie. That's what revenge-killings/suicides are: reductions of the mystery of life to one theatrical, maudlin fling. It's a Hollywood society.

▲

For a long time I was afraid that I'd just fall into line, get a good job, have a family. But in what context would my kids be raised, what social environment? Through what cultural vision would they navigate? That might is right, that the strongest and richest thrive, that what is good for the Gross National Product is good for the masses? I never could take that step. Instead, I became a martial artist, a self-proclaimed seeker of truth. Unfortunately, I was too angry to get into society, yet also too committed to live totally outside it or be able to tear it all down. "Martial artist" was about the only occupation that caught my imagination. The martial arts are not about violence; they are the antidote to violence, the antidote to anger, the antidote to fear. I trained attention; I trained powers; I trained skills. But there weren't a lot of job openings in the Help Wanted.

Training myself was the first step, and I learned, even as an angry, young, displaced man, that:

You can't blame your parents for how you act.

You can't blame your boss.

You can't blame it on guns.

You can't blame women.

You can't blame men.

You can't blame the ruling class.

You can't blame big business.

lead groups and do one-on-one things. There I learned even more about Gestalt and other therapies.

I had found my new philosophy. I had been a long-hair vegetarian doing yoga and now I had this. Plus I was developing political attitudes. I felt betrayed by my country. The teacher's arguments countering capitalism seemed obviously true to me. Minnesota, in general, however, felt less welcoming than the communities in college and Minneapolis that surrounded me. My teacher had belonged to the Communist Party, as I mentioned. The actual CP, not some other leftist group. I never went to any of the meetings, but he made me aware of all the contradictions of capitalism and all that Marxist stuff. Which I loved. I did join the YSA, the Young Socialist Alliance, but that turned out to be very hard for me. There were a lot of arm-chair socialists who liked to sit around and intellectualize everything and get in arguments. I wasn't that much of an intellectual about it all. They knew all the subtle differences between the theories of Lenin and Trotsky, all the details, and I didn't. I went to an annual conference of the YSA in Milwaukee one year. Didn't have fun at all. Everyone was very serious and argumentative. It was really easy to see how the left wing in this country had no chance of getting anything together.

I was never involved in any of the protest movements. But I really did feel betrayed by the US government. This was a feeling that developed while I was in college, though it had its seeds while I was in the army. At that time I didn't have intellectual reasons for it, but I saw a lot of waste. This was during the early '70s, remember. At the end of my time in the army there was that fuel shortage on, but every morning we'd start up all the trucks—just about all the trucks on our compound, and I'm sure all the other compounds were doing it too—hundreds of trucks were left to run for about fifteen minutes for what they called "combat readiness." Great clouds of diesel smoke enveloped what must have been the whole state—every morning.

Another wasteful practice was how they dealt with food. If they misjudged how much food was going to be eaten on a particular day, they'd just throw trays and trays and trays of perfectly good food away. There was just a lot of waste.

After college I got a job at the Burnsville Youth Center. I watched the kids, played football and ping-pong with them, and made sure they didn't break anything. Most of them were runaways, often with drug "problems." Working with those kids I woke up to how easily something else can be blamed instead of the central problem. The central problem was not taking responsibility for one's own behavior. The staff did most of the blaming, and they blamed the drugs. Most of the staff were ex-drug users or ex-alcoholics themselves, twelve-steppers, and

26

they were very afraid of drugs and alcohol. They would be at work and they'd be drinking gallons of coffee with pounds of sugar—more substances to take the place of those they'd lost control over. It had to be something else, something besides not abusing controlled substances that was the key to health. I was still into Ram Dass's *Be Here Now* and Yoga; I was still experimenting with LSD. I had other ideas.

A few of us there were into gestalt therapy, as I had been from my earlier work. We were putting our kids into trances, having them lie down on the floor— "imagine you're on an elevator and going ten floors down. When the door opens, you'll be in a whole other world...." They thought it was great. Eventually I led groups of kids.

After the Army I joined a Tae-Kwon-Do class in Bloomington. I should say I joined a series of classes because I went through about eight teachers until I found a good one. Most were Americans; a few were Koreans. This one Korean master was the real thing—Moon Kyu Kim. A very impressive guy. Moon Kyu Kim epitomized everything I worshiped in martial arts. He looked good. He was really powerful. He was strong and fast. He'd have two people hold up a tennis ball in each hand and he'd do spinning kicks, which was like a flashy back kick, and just go whoof! whoof! whoof! whoof! and kick the tennis balls out. He jumped over people and broke boards—all that kind of stuff. Studying with Kim, I got a brown belt in two and a half years. However, there were some limitations to what I learned there.

I was trained in what is called "point-karate," that is, you make slight contact and then back off. We were in competition with the school down the street, a Jhoon Rhee school. We were taught to look down on them for being untraditional, but the truth was that they actually put on gloves and made this stuff work!

I also worked a lot in health-food stores, especially during the '80s in Minneapolis. The juice bar was my specialty. I supported my martial arts training by making healthy drinks.

One day I was out on a bike ride with my beautiful hippie girlfriend, and some guys drove by in a loud car. First they harassed her, then they drove back and threw a beer can at me. I gave them the finger. They jumped out of the car.

As one guy came at me, I gave him the perfect round kick right in the solar plexus. The trouble was, I barely touched him. I had done a lot of sparring, but it was all just touch and back off. I got the guy pissed off and he jumped on me. I knew enough moves so that I didn't get badly hurt, but I was thoroughly humiliated. I had never felt fear like that before. I never had been faced with violence like that before.

I had never studied fear, so I just panicked. I had no

idea what a real fight was about. It was a little epiphany about martial arts. I never had felt fear like that before.

It was a totally new experience for me. I realized that something was missing from my martial arts training. It was a big thing, this matter of dealing with fear—what to do, how to act under duress. The way I was studying martial arts in Minnesota wasn't working for me. I realized I had to move to California and decide whether I wanted to be an Aikido guy, a T'ai Chi guy, or become a Rolfer and the hell with the whole martial thing.

It took me three months to decide to break up with my girlfriend and actually make the move. It was one of the truly sad events of my life, but I was fed up with Minnesota and it seemed that everything was happening in California—martial arts, but also Rolfing, Gestalt Therapy, hypnosis. If I was going to do martial arts, I couldn't just be a *pretend* martial artist; I had to make the stuff I was learning real. I packed my car and drove out West.

This was in 1976. I didn't have much of a sense of Berkeley as a place at first. Of course, everyone had heard of Berkeley, but I don't think I was even aware that it was in the Bay Area. When I first got to California, I lived with somebody that I'd known in the army, Duane. We lived in the "Hood" in Oakland—a very dangerous neighborhood. He was a white guy, but he'd been raised there. We lived together for about six months. I had brought my beautiful custom-built bicycle with me to California, because I was really into bicycling at the time. I rolled all over the place, and one day I found myself in Berkeley. There I was on Telegraph Avenue, and Bang! It changed my life. I hung out on the Avenue, ate my first meal at Bongo Burgers, and about three days after I found Berkeley I was living there. And that was when I faded out from Duane and met Norris.

Norris was a huge man, physically, intellectually, emotionally. We met at the school and hit it off. He had a room he wanted to rent out, and as soon as I realized I wanted to be in Berkeley, poof! I moved in with Norris. Norris was a classic Berkeley hippie, a Berkeley intellectual Hippie. Very politically oriented. He spent a lot of time in Central and South America. It was very dangerous, and he almost got killed several times. So I was living with Norris and we became great friends. He was a little bit off, but we got along fine. We lived together a couple of years, and then we just drifted apart. More about Norris later.

▶

The first place I studied was the Wen Wu School on St. Pablo Avenue in Berkeley. The teacher was in the Yang family T'ai Chi lineage, not the lineage of Yang Chen Fu but Yang Pan Hao. An old legend about this branch of the Yang family was that if, after a hundred days, you wanted to study with Yang Pan Hao, you had to be able to stand there with your weight on one leg and your chin touching the big toe of your extended other leg. If you couldn't or wouldn't do that, you couldn't be his student. Of course, we didn't have to do that, but being able to bring your chin to your toe, because of that legend, was a big deal in that school. And I saw a lot of people who were able to do that. It was the funniest thing you ever saw in your life.

The real meaning of this legend was that this school gave a lot of thought to preparation before you started to learn combat styles and methods. The first six months of training there was just Chi Kung, stretches, and other calisthenics. I lasted about three months because what I wanted to do was fight. Now I wish I had done more of that kind of stuff. But I made a lot of friends. I met Norris, the guy that I lived with in Berkeley for years. When I quit, I went looking for what else was out there and found Peter Ralston's Chen Hsin school on Telegraph Avenue.

The first time I showed up, Peter Ralston, the teacher, wasn't there. What I saw didn't impress me, so I left with no intention of going back. Then I got a job at Eden Natural Foods on University, and the manager there at the time, a guy named Russ, said, "You've got to go back to the Cheng Hsin School and see Peter. Until you see Peter himself in action, you don't know what Cheng Hsin really is."

So I went back when Peter was there. I met him and told him I'd like to study both T'ai Chi and Hsing-I at the same time, and he said, "Okay. No problem." Now that was unusual. Other teachers wouldn't have let me do that. You had to learn one martial art, and that was it.

After I started to study with Peter, I didn't see anything uniquely special about him, at least at first. He was just someone who let me do Hsing-I along with my T'ai Chi. A few weeks into the class I decided to check him out more closely. I asked him if he wanted to play. He said, "Okay." He jibed at me, saying that Tae-Kwon-Do people like me really can't kick.

Because of his listening skill, he mastered the distance, just stepping out and stepping in, and prevented me from throwing any of my kicks. Just normal stuff, as I know today, but at the time I thought it was magic. I was enthralled.

Of course, there was a lot more to Peter than preventing Tae-Kwan-Do kicks, because Peter was actually teaching about mind. He was interested not only in how you fought with your skills and your weapons, but what you did with your attention, how you located yourself in the fight, and how you practiced. It was awareness training and boxing coming together. The Karate Kid was being shown into the League.

Peter said some amazing things. He made me realize that fighting was about my whole being. A punch had all this stuff behind it—mind, energy, position, emotion, unconscious mind—even ontology. Dodging a punch involved all this too.

Many of us deny our violence, the violence within each of us; that's why it's so fearful. We are afraid to look at and be responsible for our ability to do harm. A martial art worthy of violent situations is one in which the matters of fear, violence, and responsibility have been looked into. Training this way isn't Tae Bo, and it isn't kickboxing; it's awareness training, and it can be very intense.

With all these issues as part of the training, Peter didn't present himself as just some martial arts instructor. He had no problem with people thinking of him as a guru. This wasn't *necessarily* a bad thing. We were young men looking for initiation, and here was this guy doing all this cool Carlos Castaneda mindfulness boxing stuff. He was a great teacher, very dangerous and scary. And his boxing classes were dangerous and scary. One time, a group of his other students ripped him off of me because they thought he was going to kill me. He wasn't. I'm sure he knew what he was doing. But he would take it that far. Looking back, I'm sure there would be lawyers waiting outside of his door today. But back then, it was a hard school. A great school.

I liked the depth of Peter's teaching. Because true warriorship isn't just boxing or doing sets of exercises or sitting in meditation: it's life itself. We crave this kind depth and meaning, and it's tragic that self-exploration can seem frivolous and narcissistic.

One day Peter came in and said, "I'm here and you're there." We all nodded, like sure. But then he repeated it: "I'm here and you're there." We nodded again, maybe laughed a little. He said, "I'm here and you're there." Suddenly we got kind of nervous, wondering what he meant. "I'm here and you're there. That's the single most important thing, and I'm going to keep repeating it until you get it."

Now what he was doing was showing us how critical feeling distance and placement are, exactly the magic he used when he and I played together the first time. If I had known that stuff, I wouldn't have used my great round kick on that guy who threw the beer can at me. I would have established my distance and position, stepping in and stepping out. I would have frustrated him and then turned his own energy against him.

Of course, take it a step, and I never would have given the finger; it never would have happened; we would have made friends or something; but then maybe I wouldn't have moved to California.

Another time, Peter was talking about punches and how we get totally fixated on, say, the arm. He asked us how we were experiencing our arm, right then, without looking at it. He explained that it's not a visual image but a sensation. He started us feeling each punch in the sensation of the arm before we formed any concept and started any action.

Peter's big thing was to understand what was actually happening—not the drama of the fight, not some image of being a great warrior, but the simple physical, mental reality. He said, "When you get in trouble, you get in trouble because of what came before you got in trouble." That is, before we even thought the fight had begun. And that's true. What we believe and think is happening generally determines the outcome.

"What comes before you get in trouble? What your opponents know and what they don't know are critical for determining what they will do. What can't they handle just by the very fact that they are standing? What will they react to? What they will react to will be in large measure relative to what they know."

This was heady stuff but, as we practiced it every day, the results were incredible. Peter told us to neutralize an attack by, in the same moment, becoming it. He was saying that we defeat an opponent by joining him. Only we don't defeat him so much as become a single experience with him, one thing, not him and me. You handle him simply because you have a relationship with him, and you understand it, while he only understands something else which isn't happening. This changes the whole meaning from the Hollywood sense of a fight as being pure opposition to this whole new thing.

Peter also said: "In the domain where we are not trying to win, winning is like a side effect. It's not like it isn't a goal, not like you are not participating, not like you are trying to lose; it's not that. You must fully participate, but without concentrating on winning. In Cheng Hsin, as you try to study the principles, you will fail to do them, you will move in and out of them, and you will learn."

This was what we were cultivating—purity of being and pure attention to each other's being.

In practice, there were situations where winning definitely *was* a part of it. When I joined Cheng Hsin, Peter was training for the World Championship in Taiwan. This was the best time to study with him, then and right afterwards. He said he was going to win the whole thing. I thought, "This cocky golden boy from California was going to get his ass kicked."

Peter did go to Taiwan, and he did fight. And he won. Like he said, he won everything. He did very, very well. He came back, and he was very passionate about communicating everything he knew about martial arts. He was very hungry and willing, and I was a great student. I studied, trained things over and over until I knew them inside out. Peter always said that the difference between him and us was that he had practiced a move maybe ten thousand times, so, when he did it again in a fight, it was nothing special. We had to get to where sensations of fear and anger were so much less than our mastery of the move, our internal feeling and appreciation of it. That made us very dangerous fighters.

I was in California that first time for four years, and most of my time there was studying with Peter Ralston. And I met Joanne, the woman that I married. She was going to the Lomi School, which was, at the time, a premier, cutting edge bodywork school. So we were both students, doing exactly what we wanted to do in exactly the right place. We were very much in love and it was great. We supported ourselves at entry-level jobs at healthfood stores. I basically worked, studied, rode my bicycle, and gave all my money to Peter! Eventually I started teaching, while I was still studying. It wasn't at his school, but it was with his permission, though it got some people angry. He had me helping other students after a point, and then there was an apprenticeship program, so I did that for a while.

A year or so after Peter's victory in Taiwan, we put together a boxing team to go to Hawaii to fight in another big tournament for the glory of Cheng Hsin. About eight of us started training. We trained every day very hard, we read Peter's manual, had study groups, and did a lot of boxing.

While preparing for the upcoming world tournament, Peter organized what he called "An Enlightenment Training," and it both confirmed and changed the way I saw myself and others.

The "team" met at a house in the Oakland Hills. Of course, Peter was there, and he introduced us to "The Enlightenment Master." I've forgotten his name.

He told us the purpose of the training was to have "an enlightenment experience." I got excited. The specific goal was "to directly experience who you are" and to communicate that to another.

We formed two lines facing each other and sat on the floor. One would "ask" his partner a question, just once, clearly and with strong intention, and the "asker," with interest, would listen to the answers for three minutes, and then the Master would hit a bell and we would switch roles.

The question was simply, "Tell me who you are." Then there were three minutes for the answer, and the answer was "ongoing" for those three minutes, like a "free association." For example:

"Tell me who you are."

Answer: "I'm Ron Sieh. I'm human. I'm a man. I'm here. I'm an experience," *Et cetera*, like that…answering as the questions come up.

This was a three-day event, all day every day into the night. During the first day I was running out of answers, and again the master would say, "Directly experience who you are and communicate that to your partner."

The Master was an awake guy (at least in that context; I didn't know if he was awake when he was stuck in traffic). He could tell if what I was saying were more intellectual answers or direct experience. In fact, I thought I had it on the first day, *ta DAH!*, so I *did* communicate that to my partner, and I got a private meeting with the Master and told him my answer. He simply said, "I don't believe you."

Well...I had run out of answers. I went through the night and continued all the next day to try to experience who I was. (I remember Peter whispering in my ear the morning of the second day, "You're at a building that has no windows, no doors, and you need to get inside.")

Late on the second day I directly experienced who I was (am). No Big Deal. I told the master. He said, "That's true," and he gave me another question to answer: "Tell me what life is."

You're probably wondering what I said, but if I told you, it would just be words. I said pretty much the same thing I did on the first day; only then it was an intellectual event.

Eventually four of us went to Hawaii. This tournament in Hawaii itself was a scary affair. It was a tournament where people routinely got hurt, where people have even died. There's no protective gear. You can't hit anybody in the head, but you can *kick* them in the head. There's no grappling, but you can break somebody's knee. It ended up a big debacle and a letdown.

The first night there Peter and one of my fellow students got into a big fight. On the plane flight, some place between San Francisco and Hawaii, they changed his weight category from heavy-weight to infinity! Somehow word came that the tournament had changed it. "Infinity" was an actual category. It meant, obviously, that anybody could be in it who was heavier than heavy-weight. The student, whose name was Bob, didn't want to fight these huge Summo type guys, so Peter had a big verbal fight with Bob. Peter used all his coercive skill as a teacher to guilt him into fighting, but Bob was smart enough to say, "No, I'm not going to fight a 400 pound guy when I weigh 200 pounds." So he quit. Then, just before the first fight that I was supposed to compete in, Peter announced that he was leaving Hawaii and going back to California. He had some sort of family reunion back home. Everything having to do with the tournament became tainted after that. A student named Hal was supposed to fight first, but in the wake of Peter's announced departure we were all a bit demoralized. Hal fought and lost, and then I was to fight. People got killed in these things, this was no joke. I felt totally betrayed. Through the whole thing, Peter was going to fight and lead the team, and he didn't. So he lied. A lot of my

Vroom Vroom !!! for the glory of Chen Hsin went away after that.

I lost my fight, which itself was a bit of a joke. All the referees were Asian. If you weren't Asian, you had to almost kill the guy you were fighting to win a round. My morale was gone. I was matched against the Korean national champion. So I lost the first round. It was a match that took place within the circle of a wrestling mat. And one of the things I learned was that you've got to read the rule book. It turned out that every time you stepped out of the circle you got two points off. And the referees kept raising their hands and yelling every time I stepped outside of the circle. I didn't know what it was about. So I lost it on points. That's what I like to think. I thought I did pretty well. I even thought I won that first round, but in fact I lost, so I thought, "Fuck this," and I stopped trying. Then I lost the second round, too. I went home.

In spite of Hawaii, Peter was a wonderful teacher. It's just that you can't make a martial artist into a guru. Maybe even gurus can't remain gurus for long.

I studied with Peter another three months after Hawaii. Then I went back to Minnesota feeling angry and betrayed. This was in 1980. Joanne came with me, but the first winter killed us. We stayed married for a total of four and a half years. We had been married in Berkeley for about a year, and about three years in Minnesota.

As soon as I got back to Minneapolis I started my own T'ai Chi school. I taught T'ai Chi, push-hands, Hsing-I, and a big fancy set called "Lokap." I did that for a long time, ten years in fact, all through the '80s. I had my own building for two years, but I taught in various locations—YMCAs, rented spaces. At the same time I worked at health-food stores, including long stints in Minneapolis at juice bars, first at a place called Tao Foods, then at Nutrition World. That's also when I wrote most of my first book, *T'ai Chi Ch'uan: The Internal Tradition*.

At that time I had a very elitist attitude about martial arts: what I do is the best; what everybody else does sucks. I even went around and challenged other T'ai-Chi teachers in Minneapolis. This is, traditionally, what martial arts teachers are supposed to do to make the martial arts stronger. But I didn't get very far here. Everybody refused. They didn't want to fight. Fighting was beneath them, plebian stuff. So I got the reputation of being a hard-assed T'ai-Chi guy.

My attitude was tough because I felt betrayed and angry. The reality was that Cheng Hsin was simply a very hard school. Now, looking back, I think Cheng Hsin was borderline abusive, but because of that so-called abuse, I saw parts of myself that I would never have seen otherwise, and I went places in martial arts that most people never go. They just don't get into it that deeply.

A

As I mentioned, when I first came back to Minneapolis from San Francisco, People were teaching T'ai Chi there, but none of them did what I did—which was not just T'ai Chi, but T'ai Chi *Ch'uan*—that is, put on gloves and treat T'ai Chi as a real fighting art. We actually boxed. "Ch'uan" can mean "fist," but it can also mean real boxing. All the principles of T'ai Chi—relax and sink and unify and use your whole body and be sensitive and blend—you'd bring all that into an arena with gloves and mouth pieces. William C.C. Chen teaches this in New York, but very few other T'ai Chi teachers do. T'ai Chi in the U.S. is mostly for health, and it's like a dance. One of Peter's great lines after boxing class was, "Get the blood off the floor, we've got a T'ai Chi class coming in."

◀

To compete with so-called T'ai Chi teachers, I realized that you had to be an entrepreneur. In all my training I hadn't done anything like that. I hadn't done martial arts training to be a *merchant*. I did martial arts to be a member of "the warrior class." But I learned pretty quickly that the best merchant wins. You can't get out of that here. That's the current state of the world—what happens when the merchants are in control. It's a sad day when the burghers take over from the samurai. Here we are.

So I did what I could in that regard for years. I taught in a lot of different places—a lot of WMCAs.

One day back in Minnesota I had a psychic reading. One of the many things the psychic talked about was that I had a very powerful teacher in my space, and Peter immediately came to mind. She said I had received a "utility belt" of skills in exchange for Peter being in my space. I wondered, if I took that space back, would I still keep my skills? I figured that the energy I could regain from taking responsibility for my own skill would be a worthwhile gamble. The psychic proceeded to "kick" Peter out of my space. Every time prior to this event, when I had engaged in martial arts, I always felt as if I were doing Peter's art. What the psychic did was bring this fact to my attention, and this allowed me to regain power over my own skills and energies.

4

Being Awake

I am fundamentally a meditation teacher. I teach mindfulness, and martial arts is the arena for the work. I haven't participated in anything else that gives the potent, no bullshit feedback that the study of martial arts does.

Being interested in developing awareness itself is what has always driven me in martial arts. I tell people that I'm a meditation teacher of mindfulness in the Vipassana Tradition, but the means that I've chosen is martial arts. I've never taught meditation separately. I don't have people bring a cushion and sit. I do stuff like: stand there, pick a posture, whatever posture you want, and pick a part of your body, like your hands, or the sensation of your feet on the ground, or the rising and falling of your abdomen as you breathe, whatever. Pick a part of your body and that will be your anchor. That sensation. You don't want to lose that sensation. That will be your meditation whatever you are doing. You can start doing your exercise set, and the moment you lose the sensation of, say, your feet on the floor, you stop doing the set, or whatever you're doing, get that sensation back, and continue. When you lose the sensation, for instance, if you start thinking about pizza or start daydreaming, first you've got to acknowledge that you've lost it, then you stop doing what you're doing, get the sensation back, and then continue.

This is just like traditional Vipassana meditation where you have your attention on the rising and falling of your abdomen, the sensation of that, and whenever you lose it, you can even label it, like "thinking, thinking," or "itching, itching," or whatever it is that has captured your attention, and then go back to the sensation of your abdomen rising and falling. You can bring that into your set. You can pick a part of your body. I would even do that in the context of push hands or boxing, because it's really easy to lose it when you're faced with somebody in a competition or a real fighting context. You can leave your body or just wish you weren't around. It's easy to lose the sensation of the body, so I continually create situations for students to bring themselves back to sensation.

The way energy is is that I feel it in the body. I just get more and more sensitive. It's not like I feel my body and then my experience of energy is something else. It's rather a refined sensation in my body. So to find a way to keep bringing attention back to the sensation in the body is awesome in the martial arts.

The big picture of mindfulness practice is number one: Noticing if you are awake or on autopilot; and number two: Sustaining that noticing.

"Awake" is simply that. The best way to consider "awake" is to think of it as waking from a dream. The central quality of a dream is our lack of control. We are spectators. We don't consider that we have choices concerning how we behave. "Waking up" in a dream (lucid dreaming) allows for choices. Being lucid in the "waking world" allows for choices as well. Being "asleep in the waking world" denies us choices.

Being awake is choosing not to be asleep. There is a quality of vigilance about it, and, with that, a deepening sense of responsibility, and, with that, personal power. This is not the petty personal power used to manipulate others in order to get what you want, but the power that comes with choosing how to be, who to be, how to act.

I can tell you, after teaching martial arts and mindfulness for decades, that it's effortless to live in a fantasy world of our own creating. We move in and out of a trance state. I define "trance" as being disengaged from the world of relationship and being wholly internal. It is like being in a dream and being unaware you are in a dream. In a trance you exist in and through your thoughts of the world rather than through being in the world.

In the pictures in our own minds, we can do anything: visit other worlds, heal, kill, turn into a dragon and fly away, have sex, be rich, anything. It's a fantasy life. Creativity is born here and thoughts of self-improvement as well, but also thoughts of shooting people you don't like.

Being a *Star Trek* fan, I know about the Holodeck and Holodeck addiction. The Holodeck is the ultimate programmable virtual world with touch, taste, sound, and smells. It's as interactive as you wish. You can even eat the food and drink the wine; it all tastes like food and wine. And just think of the sex, the combat, the adventures and exploration anywhere in the known universe. Any environment, all real. Well, you know.

In our so-called "real" world, today, if you're having trouble making friends, you jump into a chat room. If you're having trouble finding a sexual relationship, jump into a sexual chat room or have a virtual, real-time sexual encounter via computer with a "real" person—but be sure your Visa is ready.

I've read that mice given the choice between pushing a button and getting a pellet of food and pushing another button and getting some cocaine will starve high on coke.

❥

We all have an internal state. What I mean by this is not

a trance, but our personal experience, our interior life, how we experience our selves, our body, our mind, our emotions, and our spirit. This is where the true game is played, in our selves, not on any computer screen. This is where we can play for real and have great adventures.

The world in front of us can crumble and transform into a splendiferous dragon surrounded by the crackling power of creation and destruction. All "secrets" revealed and truth made manifest. But it will only happen and last for the blink of an eye. If we are not awake, we'll miss it.

The last walk I went on was in Wisconsin. I came upon a deer carcass. It looked like it had been killed and eaten—coyotes? a wolf?—a mystery. I scared up a turkey. I saw bald eagles. The wood ticks were out, and ducks, geese, kingfishers, new flowers, good air, good company. Wholesome fare! Better than sitting in a cubicle, staring at a cathode-ray tube.

What a judgment!

This notion that judging is bad. That's incorrect. Without discriminating intelligence there is no intelligence. $2 + 2 = 5$ isn't a good guess, it's wrong. Being nice is better than being cruel; saying something is better than taking abuse. It's better to take responsibility for your actions than to blame others. It's better to communicate than to be passive aggressive, or steam till you blow up. Relaxed is better than tense, power is superior to strength, timing is more important than speed. Look both ways before you cross the street, and don't call King Kong a monkey.

Wholesome is a good barometer for our behavior. Is what we are up to wholesome and satisfying or not? Wholesome is what is beneficial and healing—beneficial and healing to ourselves and to others. Go ahead, ask yourself if what you spend your time doing is beneficial and helpful. From the food you eat, to how you treat yourself, to what you do for entertainment, to how you treat others, to how you make money, to how you spend it, everything is open to investigation and the application of mindfulness.

When I hear people complain about the circumstances in their lives (I'm overly experienced at this myself), there is a sense of helplessness that is as "real" as the circumstances that give cause of the complaining. We may think we are the victims of circumstance, but we are actually the victims of our own sense of helplessness. Also we take it for granted, as if there were no alternative. This way of being, of avoiding pain, seeking pleasure, of suffering and grasping after fleeting gratification, is called Samsara in the Buddhist tradition.

The first step in finding alternatives to being caught up in the whirlwind of circumstances is to create some space, some emotional and psychic space, between you and the world. By emotional and psychic space I don't mean for you to be insensitive and unfeeling or to armor up against what causes you pain. You need to create space between the circumstance and the blind knee-jerk reaction that follows it.

The practice of creating space is called mindfulness. Without it we are denied the opportunity of choosing how to act. When we are only in reaction to our world, our actions reflect it. We are offended by the actions of others. We feel disrespected all the time.

The next time someone angers or disrespects you, instead of letting the program take over, acknowledge the anger to yourself. Simply say, "Hey, here's that mind state again. Far out. I'm pissed. How am I going to act?" Instead of giving the finger or plotting revenge, acknowledge the anger and choose to be free in relation to it.

If we want to stop spreading around violence, it is essential we be awake enough to see its creation long before it has turned into facedowns and drive-by shootings. How do we move from perception to judgment to action? It takes just a flicker, a few nanoseconds—damn fast. So fast that its components are blurred. Yet our life hangs in the balance in situations like this. Every situation provides an opportunity to train awareness. With awareness, life becomes interesting again. Our attention is in demand at every moment. The study becomes real, down-to-the-bones real. For a person who's made the choice to train consciously in awareness, the matter of being awake is as much a conscious choice as a matter of need. We want to be aware, especially when it's not "needed."

We need to create space between the circumstance and the blind knee-jerk reaction that follows it. Developing a meditation practice doesn't have to be a big deal. In fact, it can be woven into one's life in such a way that, to an observer, what we're up to wouldn't appear much different from before. In mindfulness meditation we want to be aware of thoughts as thoughts, sensation as sensation, emotions as emotions. We don't want to attach anything to these. We simply want to recognize them, to be aware of ourselves as we are. We want to make a distinction between present time and the past or future, or between our hopes and fears about the future and how events that happened in the past have momentum behind them.

Meditation is a chance to be who you are—behind all the stuff going on in your mind. In meditation you can feel anger, revenge, desire, lust, jealousy, greed, and all the rest of that good stuff. But you just have to notice it, like birds moving on the horizon or cars going by. You're not at the mercy and service of all your thoughts and emotions. It's because you're really the boss, and you get to choose how to act.

5

Back to California

After ten years in Minneapolis, I went back to California to study martial arts and other things in more depth.

I went to California on a vacation and decided that I wanted to move back. While I was there, I answered an ad in a newspaper that said a guy named Larry had a room in his house to rent. Larry seemed like a nice guy. He was a psychologist. The house was pretty messy by Minnesota standards—there can be a kind of sloppiness to California, comparatively, when it comes to things like keeping the bathrooms clean—but he seemed okay, so I arranged to live there. In about two weeks I finished up my business in Minnesota, packed up my little Mazda, and drove to California to live with Larry.

When I arrived, my first stop was Norris's house. He was still there, still Norris, but he had gone through some difficult times. He had gotten a law degree at I think it was New College Law School. It was a very left-wing law school, and he was now a well-trained lawyer, but like me he had no entrepreneurial spirit, no business sense. He wasn't interested in starting a business, so he was failing fast. He was much more emotionally distraught than I had ever seen him, but we hung out for a while and then eventually we fell apart again, and I haven't seen him for a long time. But if it wasn't for Norris . . . . When I got to California I didn't have any money. When I visited Norris he had this huge jar of change—not pennies—and he said, "Ron, if you take this huge jar to the bank you can keep the money." And I did—it was about two hundred bucks. That really helped me for my first couple of weeks.

So I was living with Larry, but after about a week, I just couldn't stand the guy any more. I was very jugmental. At that time I was a vegetarian and I worked out a lot, and he wasn't a vegetarian and he didn't work out at all, so we didn't have much in common. We didn't have much to say to each other, and the house was a dump, so I just hung out in my little room. He usually made noise at night, and most nights I'd have to get up and tell him to be quiet, but then, one night—something happened. He *was* quiet. Then, for the next three or four days I didn't hear anything. And I thought it was great! Wow! Maybe he's gone! I didn't know what was going on. But then on about the fourth day, his nephew, whom I'd met on several occasions, showed up and said that earlier that morning he had gone into Larry's bedroom and there he was, lying on his bed with his mouth open, and a couple of flies buzzing about it. And that was why the house was so quiet. Because Larry was dead.

One day before his death, he had told me he couldn't "feel" his back. I'd done some bodywork at that point so I gave his back a feel. There was something there, all right. It felt like a piece of wood. I touched it and recoiled, and I said, "I don't know what the hell that is, Larry, but you got to get it looked at," and about a week and a half later he was dead. He was in his early fifties. I don't know if they did an autopsy.

When I got to California this second time, it was very hard to find employment. I did temp work that was literally digging ditches. It was kind of funny because my dad always said unless you go to vocational school or finish college you're going to end up digging ditches. And here I was, digging ditches, usually for a crew of carpenters, and I was the low man on the team. Eventually I got a full time job with a crew of carpenters, but I was still the low man—the "gopher," going back and forth between the lumber yards and the work place. One of the things I found out pretty quickly was that just being in the Bay Area didn't mean that I was outside of the world of macho, hierarchy-oriented people. Working for those guys was not fun. If I ever made a mistake, it slowed up the whole crew, because I was the guy who went and got the materials. If they made a mistake, no big deal, they'd get a new piece of lumber and do it over again. But if I screwed up, the whole project was on hold, and everybody let me know it.

One of the first jobs I did was at the home of Richard Grossinger, the publisher of North Atlantic Books. I remember his son, Robin, remarked on how poorly the carpenters treated me. He was used to me being this kung fu guy that got a lot of respect and that you paid money to to get private lessons, and here I was the low man on the carpenter team getting kicked around. So that was one of the worst jobs I ever had.

Another "worst job" was driving a truck for a bread factory called "Uprisings Bakery" in Oakland. Uprisings was a Collective. Getting trained was okay, learning about the bakery was okay, but once my probation period was over and I started fulltime, I made an enemy. There's something about overweight, middle-aged women. They don't like me. This one hated me. Since it was a collective, there weren't many bosses; in fact, there weren't *any* bosses, but this woman, Joanne, acted like a boss. I was new, and she singled me out as the person whose life she was going to make a living hell. But I did the job, and one of the things I found out really quickly was that in a collective, even if it's a relatively "utopian" system, if it's full of angry people, it goes to hell. There are slackers and people who care, and the people who care make up for the slackers, but the anger goes around and doesn't dissipate.

Never work for a collective. Socialism is a grand idea, but nothing ever got done at Uprisings because everything worked on pure consensus. If one person disagreed, nothing would happen. And one person always disagreed.

While on that job I slowly developed a serious injury. I had to pick up a lot of one or two pound loaves of bread. If you reach down, palm down, and pick up a loaf of bread too many times, it overworks the extensors in your forearm. I got tendonitis so bad I couldn't pick up a pint of beer with my right hand. After a while I was going back and forth between work and the doctor, who wouldn't do anything but give me ibuprofen and send me back to work. He wanted me to get a cortisone shot, but I kept putting it off and never got it. Eventually the ibuprofen stopped being effective and I couldn't work.

Working at Uprisings was toward the end of my second time in California. I'll pick up what happened after I was injured in a little while.

Once I was settled in at Larry's, I started almost at once to study with Randy Cherner, who became one of my most important teachers. Randy doesn't do *body*work as opposed to, say, *mind*work or *spirit*work. He has a very fluid, unbounded sense of the body, the mind, the chakras, the aura. The act of touching another person is a deep act, and he communicates how to do that so that you are simultaneously contacting the aura and the physical being of the other person. Then your touch just melts through the muscular space. Even as it contacts the unexpected stickiness and turbulence of the aura, it dissolves through actual flesh. Cultivating this skill can serve well in healing and equally well in fighting. In fact, Randy is an aikidoist and athlete as well as a bodyworker.

At the time I met him, what Randy taught was so simple that I really didn't appreciate it. He was interested in where you contact the other person's field, how touch changes things, and who's feeling what. I only studied one year with him, but during that time he kept saying, "If you just learn to deeply feel yourself in relationship and feel the body that you're touching, that's good enough for now." I wish I had studied with him longer.

Later I studied with a number of bodyworkers who had none of that subtlety of approach and who just cultivated techniques. How you cross somebody's boundaries, who you are, who they are wasn't even spoken of. Randy kind of wrecked me for other teachers, but he prepared me for a larger universe in which "emotional" and "psychic" are inherently part of the physical. You can feel them in the field around the body, and you can feel them in the body.

Randy helped turn me from a martial artist into a healer; he showed how the same skills that enabled me to do damage could be cultivated to cure. That is, after working with Randy, I could feel and shift people's energies; I could track down the sources of their blocks and release them.

Randy would have somebody in class just lie down on the floor and take a position; then one day he turned to me and said, "Ron, lay down on the floor and take that position." So I did that. And then he said, "Do you know how many people can do that? Do you know how rare a skill that is?" For me it was easy to imitate a position, but that's because it was an offshoot of stuff I had been training for years.

▲

One of the reasons I returned to California was to study martial arts in a lot more depth. In just five or so years I learned three times as much martial arts as I already knew. I was given all the twelve Hsing-I animals by Wong Jackman. At the same time, I learned the twelve-animal, two-person set called An Sum Pao. Wong Jackman also taught me Hsing-I sword and T'ai-Chi sword. I learned the long Yang T'ai-Chi set of Yang Chang-Fu from Wong Jackman too.

I studied with Wong about two, two and a half years. He is a very stoic Chinese guy. There was absolutely no free play. I had a girl friend at the time, Gloria, who was also a martial artist. We'd walk in the doorway of the school, catch Wong's eye, and bow to him. Then we'd be in class. That's where we'd do our own study. Whatever he taught us prior to that, we would work on and practice. Eventually he'd come around and acknowledge us, decide if he was satisfied with what he saw us doing, and then teach us the next few moves. He would spend maybe fifteen minutes with each of us and then go away.

These were two-hour classes, and the rest of the time we'd just study what he taught us. He did this with everybody. He wasn't that much interested in whether you did it right or not, so beginners had a very hard time at Wong's. It was a terrible place for them, because he'd never correct them. He'd never do any kind of explanation.

Now, there are twelve individual animals in Hsing-I, as I mentioned, so there are twelve "baby" sets, each quite distinct—the monkey, the dove, the hawk, the dragon, the turtle, the horse, the chicken, the tiger, the combination of eagle and bear, and so on. You learn each one really slowly, half a set each time you go to class. After I learned them all, I learned An Sum Pao, a two-person fighting set. It's choreographed, but I like choreographed stuff because you can still incorporate a lot of formless things like good timing into them.

After I learned his Hsing-I and T'ai Chi Ch'uan, I left Wong.

Then I did Filipino martial arts. First I studied with Eddie Lastra in Largomado Arnis. That ended rather quickly. Eddie didn't have a lot of techniques. In fact, after showing us the five basic strokes, he put us rather quickly in environments where we could do free play with partners.

Now, I'm a notorious trickster at free play, a regular king of the playground. Jeez, I mean, hit somebody and not get hit. I've done that before. So I found myself in a position of beating up all his students. If I were a teacher, I wouldn't have done it that way, but, as a student, I wanted to test my skills and see what I could do, what that looked like. Finally it got to the point where I was challenging the teacher, so he kicked me out of class.

That lasted maybe four or five months. Then I studied with Jeff Finder; he taught Serrada Eskrima. That worked out perfectly because he was a drill sergeant. All he trained me was technique—the whole Serrada system. It was very choreographed. So I learned the pitter-patter of Serrada, which gave me permission to do a lot of stuff that I had never done before.

Then I studied with Sonny Umpad, who was not very technique-oriented; he was much more flow-oriented. In fact, he called his own personal art "corte kadena," which means "short chain." He had respect for my stick work, so he and I did very little new of that. We did mostly what he calls "pungamoot," which is hand work, open-hand stuff and knives, and then kicking and knives together.

Sonny would teach in his small backyard, little more than a patio, just outside his kitchen. A glass sliding door separated the backyard from the kitchen and, if there were several students at a time (there would seldom be more than three), the lesson would go back and forth between kitchen time and working out. He would also have his VCR camera recording everything. Sonny was the first teacher I had who would spend time going over tapes with students. Great feedback and now great memories.

A lot of what I did with Sonny was just watch what he did. That gave me permission to do stuff that I had never even considered. He was very informal, very different from my other Eskrima teachers. A lot of times we'd just sit around the table, and he'd smoke cigarettes, drink coffee, and talk. Or we'd go out to the laundry and do a load or two.

Sonny pretty much taught me how to fly. With a stick. And with a knife. It was exciting just to be around him. He was egotistical and proud. *Very* egotistical and *very* proud. In fact, he would often get into fights with his students over some really strange things. One of his students was left-handed. Sonny had such a hard time teaching him to work right-handed that he almost challenged him to a fight. With a knife, no less.

♥

I studied with Sonny until I left California the second time. Why I left has to do with what happened to me after I couldn't work at Uprisings Bakery any more because my tendonitis.

As part of its workmen's compensation package, the State of California agreed to retrain me as a bodyworker. They gave me a little pile of money and sent me to Heartwood. Heartwood is a bodywork school in Northern California. It's a beautiful place in the mountains, maybe fifteen miles from the coast, in the Humboldt County Redwoods. Upon my arrival, one of the first things they told me was not to walk off the property because that was where some of the best marijuana in the world is grown, and the growers don't like trespassers. I was told there were a lot of bodies in those hills, belonging to people who had tried to rip off other people's pot. In fact, I heard gunfire every day. Sometimes automatic-weapons fire. There's nothing like hearing gunshots to keep you off somebody's property, so I never left the Heartwood grounds.

Because of my injury, the only bodywork that the State of California would let me learn was Polarity Therapy, which is an energy-based system—nothing really heavy like Rolfing or other more manually strenuous modalities. It's almost like acupuncture or acupressure, but it has a different outlook, based on Hindu Philosophy, which I didn't really agree with at the time, and some of it I still don't. The teacher taught Hindu Philosophy sort of on the sly. He would kind of slip stuff in there so it wouldn't sound like religion. He would say things like, "Shiva isn't a Deity, Shiva is a force of nature." He used words that had ambiguous meanings, and by this time in my life I knew what they really meant. That teacher and I didn't get along very well. He'd say something, and I'd say, "Wait a minute," and then I'd tell him what I thought he was really talking about, and it would go back and forth.

Another thing about Heartwood was that I was singled out as THE middle-aged white male, the guy that had made everything the way that it is. The reason the world sucks was because of middle-aged white guys. And by the way, Ron, you're one of them. But I did make a couple of friends.

▶

Meanwhile, I continued to study Filipino martial arts with Sonny Umpad. For the most part I dropped Chinese weapons once I discovered what Filipino arts could do. Wong Jackman, from whom I learned a couple of sword sets in San Francisco, said sword forms are like poetry. They're not like talking. Fighting is like talking. Filipino Martial arts are like talking. It's not baroque, it's not done to be pretty. I mean, they're still killing people over there with knives and sticks. The stick would be my preferred weapon, if I didn't have a gun. A stick, maybe two feet long.

Musashi, the famous samurai, who realized the use of two swords, found that when he fought a guy with a staff, the staff served as several weapons in one. Each end of the staff could be a weapon, which is very unlike a sword. I got that really clearly one day when I was playing around with sticks with Sonny. He was holding a stick in his right hand back towards his ear and the end of the stick was pointed at me. Suddenly he just reached up with his left hand and took the end of the stick that was pointed at me and now it was in his left hand and he hit me with it. I swear I actually stopped fighting, looked at him, and said to him, "You can't do that!" I thought, "Holy shit, you mean I can grab either end of this stick?" It was a big deal!

Sonny was one of the more romantic of my teachers. He lived in Alameda, a small apartment, and his walls were lined with weapons—bladed weapons, stick weapons, spears, he even had a bow and arrow. He made all this stuff himself. He took broken weapons, broken blades, and put them together into weapons. He'd always be tinkering and making this stuff. He actually didn't want to teach that much. He did it for the money to get stuff to make more weapons.

Eskrima is a form of Kali. Kali is usually considered

the Mother art in the Philippines. It was usually associated with the Muslim Filipinos. Sonny wasn't Muslim, but he was raised in a Muslim section, so he hung-out with all these Muslim kids, and he learned Muslim Kali from them. There are hundreds of thousands of styles of Kali. All these family styles, and they all keep it secret from each other.

I've never been aware of any set of specific principles in Kali, comparable to say, balance, following, blending, etc., in T'ai Chi. There is a kind of magical quality in Kali where you get more into the psychic stuff. But the teachers that I had—we never went there.

Sonny was one of those personalities that you kind of had to watch out for and cater to a bit. But he was a really skilled martial artist and a really generous man.

One of the students who eventually came to study with Sonny was a guy who taught Pa Kua and Hsing-I. Now, he and I did not get along. I mean I've really mellowed out over the years, but he was very challenging for me. He's like, "Hey, don't stick your head out too far; hey, you studied with that Peter Ralston." He dissed me for studying with Peter. He dissed my footwork. He dissed my technique. We'd work with knives and he'd be telling me how I was doing things wrong. Meanwhile I knew I could cut him to ribbons at will, if I wanted.

Then, one day at Sonny's house, I asked this guy if he wanted to do some push-hands. He was one of those really hard, strong push-hands guys, which is difficult to deal with unless you're very mobile. So I became very mobile. By this point I could work very well with my emotions. I could turn anger on and off easily and to good effect. So I turned my anger on and off, harangued him quite a bit. It turned real hard a couple of times, but nobody got hurt and it was all in good fun. But it really seemed to upset Sonny. Sonny's attitude was, "If it's aggressive, you're gonna kill somebody." If Sonny wasn't out to kill, it was totally casual and you're hardly doing anything at all. For him, it was always either hot or cold, but I've got a lot of in between, and this stuff that I did really angered Sonny because he saw it as being too aggressive.

He jumped on me the way I had seen him jump on other students in the past. He had never done that with me before. I was moving back to Minnesota anyway, so a couple of weeks later I quit studying with him.

It worked out fine. I went to say good-bye, and he was really good-humored. He said I was a great student and he was sorry to see me go. I shook hands with everybody, and he gave me a knife he made. I left. Sonny and I parted on great terms.

◀

The reason I was leaving California was that things were not working out for me financially. Once I had finished the training at Heartwood, I found myself in the same position that I had been in earlier as a martial artist. I was pretty good at doing the bodywork, the Polarity Therapy that I had been trained to do, and I've always considered myself a pretty good teacher, but I've got absolutely no entrepreneurial spirit. I have no interest at all in selling myself, and, like the martial arts gig, once I finished the training, I realized, now I've got to become a merchant. And so there I was, either having to start in another entry-level job, or start a business, and, like I say, I never had the spirit to start a business. It was an ill-conceived idea to get trained in bodywork with a profession as the end of it, but I did.

Now the benefits had run out from my injury compensation, and I was living in a friend's garage, and for the first time in my life I had no money to eat, no money to pay the rent. It didn't last long, but I'd never been there before. I'd always had a roof over my head. It was really hard.

I got totally depressed, finding myself in that position, and I thought I'd move back, so I called friends in Minnesota and told them I was starting a "Bring-Ron-Back-To-Minnesota" Grant! And my friends came through. I put all my stuff in my little Mazda GLC and drove back to Minnesota during one of the coldest winters they'd ever had in the West. I drove through Wyoming when it was ten below, but I got home, and, within a week, poof! I had a great job with the Minneapolis Park Board. I'm still working there.

I had some really intense relationships with women my second time in California. In fact, sometimes I wonder if relationships are not all real intense. That may be the nature of the beast.

But I have learned some things over the years. I think the main thing is: it's a good idea to listen to each other. Also, don't do your martial arts with your partner, either literally or figuratively.

I think it's important to find a woman who doesn't want to make everything into a challenge between herself and you. I've been through a lot of challenging women, which was originally very exciting. Fiery, on-edge, emotional, smart, strong women. Great sex. Each time the relationship lasted about two or three years.

One time I went to a Senyassin party in Mill Valley. It was idyllic: golden California, hot tubs. They were all Senyassin, Rajneesh women who are known for their sex, drugs, and rock 'n' roll. Now, I was at the party having a great time, and in walks this beautiful woman speaking in a lovely German accent. She took off all her clothes right down to her g-string. I've never been so bold in my life, but I just walked up to her and said, "I think you're beautiful, and I'd love to spend the night with you."

She said, "I just got here; let me hang out a little bit and see what I want to do. I'll get back to you."

About a half an hour later she hooked up with me and kissed me—I mean, *kissed* me. I guess she wanted to know if I was a good kisser. Ten minutes later she took me home. And that lasted for about three days.

She paid for everything, took me out to fancy restaurants, took me out to breakfast; we went for walks; had sex in beautiful places. She was like a partner in the energy of sex, a perfect opponent, and a perfect lover. And it was all about aura even at the same time as it was all about body and sex.

And she was open, the way Europeans are. She'd wake up in the morning and open the window, throw open the shutters bare-breasted, and say hi to her neighbor. It was great! He was this sixty-year-old guy cutting the grass. It made his day. A big smile on his face. "Hiiii!"

Of course, when I did my Hsing-I set, she thought it was silly; she thought I looked like a chicken. She was not into martial arts at all.

Because she was a Senyassin, she was very concerned about sexually transmitted diseases, AIDS and so on. So she had these B.F. Goodrich condoms. I've never seen anything like them. They were a condom inside a condom so that you didn't have to touch the real condom. The thing was thick, man. Other than a huge condom, it was a lot of fun. I don't even remember what her name was.

70

Now I am with a woman, Julie, who is very "us"-oriented, looking down the road years and asking, "What are 'we' going to do? How are we going to support each other?" A feminist would probably give her a lot of shit because she thinks women are better at some things and men are better at other things. Instead of challenging her man, she wants to support him. Let him be a man.

I've never been with a woman before who let me be a man. I've always been with women who wanted me to be a man the way a woman would think a man should be. As you might guess, I'm in luvvvv now. But along the way I've been through a lot.

6

Reining in the Fear

∨

I always wanted to study both magic and boxing. So, during my second stay in California, I went into the Psychic Institute in Berkeley and said, "Here I am. I'm earnest. I want to study. I want to learn this stuff." And they kicked me out. They said, "Oh, you're one of those Peter Ralston martial artists. Get out of here." They claimed I was attacking everybody with my third chakra. The teachers at the Institute said, "You've got to get control of your aura; it's blasting guys; it's rude. You're scaring people."

Well, that immediately piqued my curiosity.

One of my teachers, whom I mentioned before, Randy Cherner, said, "Ron, you have this energetic sentinel in you, always on guard and ready."

I had never really considered that before, that the foundation of my whole martial-arts passion and my huge aura and capacity for blasting people with my chakra was that I was really scared. I realized that I had wanted people to be scared of me because I was scared myself. I didn't want people to fuck with me.

Being scared isn't the worst thing; after all, the only difference between excitement and fear is a point of view. We can change our emotional states. We can realize we are moving in the wrong direction and go another way. Now I wanted to change my fear energy into another sensation so that I could train it into presence.

I'd never tried to "turn off" my scary energy; in fact, I was kind of proud of my big, intrusive, protective aura. But I was lonely and I *did* scare people. I was afraid to turn it off, but I wanted to get out of the trap I had made. I wanted to be able to make contact, real contact, with people. Scaring people was fine, but only when I wanted to, not just by showing up.

Finally, after three or four more tries at the Berkeley Psychic Institute, I gave up and went to the one in Marin. There they took me on. The guy in charge said, "Yeah, you're blasting people with your chakras and your aura's huge. Sit over there and we'll teach you how to *run your energy*." I'll give the details about what this is a little bit later. Through my studies there, I got control of my aura. I actually started to be able to pull it in.

One time while I was practicing at the Psychic Institute, I filled out my back, the space to the rear of me, with my energy. After I shifted, I had energy in my back to the same degree that I did in the front. The psychic who was monitoring me noticed the change for the better and said, "Ron, what did you do?"

I said, "I filled out my back."

She said supportively, "That's it!"

I practiced filling out, and then after that I started standing in the center of my aura instead of at its back end. Suddenly I was participating in a round energy field, actually locating myself in the center of it. And then I found I could also shrink it; I started bringing it in.

At the Psychic Institute in Marin they also teach you to put up a "protection rose" at the edge of your aura. They do a lot of work with roses because they're pretty benign. You set the rose up and you ground it. Then any negative energy that cuts toward you hits the rose first and is grounded before it gets to you.

Just to put a nice full-petalled rose at the edge of my aura, I had to know where my aura was. That was an incentive to become conscious of my aura and learn how to pull it in. Pulling my aura in changed everything.

Another of the things that they taught at the Psychic Institute was that you have to take responsibility for whatever's *inside* your aura. A lot of boundary confusions can happen if you start putting stuff that's outside you inside your aura. Not knowing what's inside your aura can make you sick.

After my trainings at the Psychic Institute I became a happier person. People weren't so scared of me. I pulled in my aura. I took responsibility for it and kept to my boundaries. I can still be really "big," but now I do it out of choice.

>

There's a bit more to say about working with fear in a combat situation. When a person finds themselves about to get into a physical fight, it is natural for there to be a good amount of fear. The first thing that anybody would have to do to deal with that fear in order to turn it to their advantage, is to acknowledge the truth of the matter. What is actually going on here? I am here, this person attacking me is here, this relationship is actually happening. And it's not going to go away. So first of all I have to acknowledge that. And under those conditions, I have to remember to breathe, to feel my body. I have to relax, acknowledge that I AM a body, and that there's another body standing there. I have to be mindful of the event—be present—that's a big thing—you've got to be present and acknowledge things as they are. It's hard to do that when the shit hits the fan. I think that's what courage is—acknowledging things as they are when you'd rather be doing something else. Dealing with it. Then when things actually start moving, like when punches are being thrown and kicks are flying, or someone tries to tackle you, instead of running or freaking out or not breathing or not feeling your body, you can just dodge the punch, step away from the kick, step away from the tackle, whatever you need to do.

Peter Ralston had a great line about fear. He said that to the degree that you are present, there is no fear. In my experience, that's pretty much true. Fear usually has to do with something that's going to happen, or something that's happened in the past, and the sense that it's going to happen again. How do you handle that? You just got to be there and do your job.

Actually, even when fear is what you are feeling, it's a pretty complex thing. When you're in a fight, of course there's a lot of aggression, and, as any psychologist will tell you, underneath that aggression is fear. But that fear is not quite the bottom line. Fear itself is already complex. Fear is based on anticipation or memory—something that your head is doing. It's a mental event. It's a mental construction. So you've got to realize the difference between this mental construction and what's actually going on. And part of what's actually going on is the adrenaline running. There's a lot of sensation, which is one of the main reasons we jump out of the body. It's typically unpleasant, so we jump out of the body and skat, psychically. But in combat you've got to be there, deal with sensation, see if you can settle things. Feel your feet on the ground. Part of the severe training—the way Peter taught and the way I teach, where your teacher really seems to be attacking you—is to get you accustomed to those physical sensations, so you can do something besides panic!

I'd had ample opportunity to watch myself freak out—in a laboratory—at the Cheng Hsin school. We would form a circle, and whoever wanted to box would jump in. You make an agreement with the person you were boxing with as to how far you want to take this, how hard you want to hit. Everybody has the agreement that you can say, "Hey, don't hit me so hard." That way you are trying to keep it relatively safe, you don't want to kill each other. You are recognizing it is still a training thing. It's different from a real, all-out fight where you are really trying to hurt each other, but still, you have ample opportunity to watch your mind, get scared, freak out, come back, get scared and freak out and come back again, and dodge the punch, get hit, and notice what the components are of dodging the punch. There's a difference psychically from what I do when I successfully dodge and when I get hit. You study what that difference is. What do I do when I dodge the punch? I've got to be in relationship. I've got to know what's going on. I've got to feel my body, and finally I've got to dodge the punch!

There was one time when I was boxing with Peter and he hit me a few times, and bam, I started crying! But he wouldn't stop, he kept hitting me. Then I started cracking jokes, which I'm pretty good at. I can get people to laugh. And that didn't work. He just kept hitting me. I started crying again. He wouldn't stop hitting me. Then I got mad at him, and told him I was going to stop studying with him. He kept on hitting me. And then eventually—I dodged the punch! I got out of the way. Holy shit! I realized that all I had to do (ha! all I had to do!) was get in relationship with this incredibly scary guy and see things as they are, and start dodging.

It's always possible to dodge. Why? Well, there's always a line of force. Whether it's a punch with a fist or a look from the eye. I discovered that in that kind of relationship I would be the target for a line of force. Which is a big realization. That I'm the target. He's not going to punch the wall or punch the ground. He's going to punch ME. But this really narrows the field. Now I know where he's going to punch. Then you know that there is a line—a train track. The target could be on your head, it could be your body, but there's really always a train track and it's there before the physical act of throwing the punch. In the beginning that's how it is. People look, choose a target, and then do something.

The line or track is a physical force. I mean, you are trained enough and sensitive enough to feel what's going on, so you feel a physical force. Even just a hostile stare is like that. There's what I call a "lock." And it works both ways. You can pick it up or send it out. I feel like that. Like "spider sense"—that kind of thing. It's a human gift. Actually, everyone can do it—we've just been trained out of it.

When Musashi was a young man, he was berated by the monk Takuan for being too loud—too loud energetically. Musashi felt dangerous to everyone around him and put everyone on edge. Someone loud can be easily read, even by the untrained. For someone trained, reading how another person runs his/her energy opens to choices that seem magical.

It's to my advantage to be quiet and hard to read. When my friend, Clint, who teaches internal martial arts in the Bay Area, and I get together, we often get into great discussions, and then he'll get excited and put a lock on me, usually while describing energetically a way of being, and I've got to tell him to point it somewhere else. It gets the hackles rising. While playing with other martial artists, I can feel when they put a lock on me and I can feel exactly where they are going to strike. If I say, "Don't you kick me!" they stop and say, "How d'you know I was going to kick you?" For them, this is kind of a magical event, but for me it's normal. I trained it.

When doing something like push-hands, the thing to know is that people always have a center of balance and they are often not aware of just where it is. At the same time, you yourself have a center of balance too. So, basically, you are both trying to find each other's center of balance. The point is knowing it: Feeling what's being targeted, and then stepping out of the way, because the attack is always a straight line. The straight line, of course, can turn into a bunch of angles, it can turn into a circle, but even a circle is really just a bunch of really tiny straight lines, so you've got to feel those lines. *Blending* is when you move in the same direction and at the same speed as the particular force that's coming at you. Walking arm in arm.

Once I can pick up the incoming force, I can create a leading quality. I am just a hair ahead of the push. I'm still offering a target, but I'm leading a little bit. All of a sudden I'm in command of the situation. I'm no longer just yielding and being at the effect of the other person. I am actually leading the person. I'm offering apples to the donkey! And once that's happening, I'm in control and I can find the exact moment to push or strike effectively or get out of the way.

The trick is that you can pick up the vector of your opponent's intent.

To blend, you have to be *interested* in what is going on. One of the things that happens when you are in a situation where you are getting beat up is that you lose interest. What happened years ago, on that fateful bike trip, was that I "left." I totally lost interest. I didn't want to be there. I left my body. Left everything. Ironically, when the heat is on, you've got to be interested. Really interested.

If somebody has a big intention to hurt me or beat me up, I've got to match that intention volume-wise. To get out of that situation, I've got to match it, or even get a little bit bigger. I don't mean match it blow by blow, anger by anger—but that I have to match the space, match the intent, not hide from it or shrink away. I've got to hold it. It's an *embracing* thing. Which is very different from in an external martial art where it's these two points fighting it out. Rather, it's like I want to embrace the person. I'm very interested. I'm asking what exactly is going on here? What motivates this person? Why is this person trying to hit me? You don't want to think thoughts like that but that's the attitude. What exactly is going on here? What can he do? What *can't* he do? Is he aware? Does he feel his back? Does he know that I am standing here? Does he even *see* me? If I step to the left, will he see me do it? How much of a gap is there between me doing it and him seeing it? If I do that, and there's a lag, then I can do whatever I want, I'm invisible, he doesn't see me.

That's the *inquiry* part. Am I relaxed? Do I feel my body? Do I feel my feet on the ground? My relationship to my own mind in that sort of a situation is like a checklist. Relaxed? yes or no. Feet on ground? yes or no. Do I feel my aura? Do I see this person? Am I in time with events as they are happening? yes or no. Instead of thinking about the circumstances and telling myself stories about what's going on, I run this checklist. What exactly is happening here? Inquiry!

❮

The difference between telling stories and running a checklist is a little bit like what I call the difference between knowing the map and knowing the territory.

Peter Ralston didn't teach any Chi Kung when I studied at his school, but the guy that I studied with for a few months before him at the Wen Wu School was all Chi Kung. Chinese medical theory in a sense is a great map—all the technique, all the knowledge. Actually being present in your body is the territory. The way I think of it is, you kind of either learn the map or you learn the territory. Mastering the instrument, getting really good at knowing your body, really inhabiting it, feeling its depths, feeling the thickness of it, feeling the textures of it, being aware of aura, being able to pull it in or make it big, mastering your sensitivity and having the ability to make that checklist so at any moment you know where you really stand—that is getting really good at the territory. Then there's the maps, learning the meridians and how they all hook up, the five element theory and the yin/yang philosophy and all the rest of Chi Kung theory. All that kind of stuff is really interesting stuff, but if that's all you've got—I'm judgmental about people who just know the map. I've met a lot of people who know recipes, but few who can cook.

Don't get me wrong. The maps are great—particularly if you've got that feeling in your body to check it out: does it really feel like its my kidney? Can you create whatever sensation you want? Can you feel the meridian if you want to?

7

Magic and Paradox

▼

I mentioned before that once I began to experience the possibilities of the martial arts, I realized that I was interested in magic. I did meet people involved in Western magic in California, but not at the Psychic Institute. My experience with Western magic came between my first and second time in California, and it is worth telling about it because it leads into some things that I did learn at the Psychic Institute and that I do want to impart here. They were, finally, more important to me than what I learned about magic.

I met a guy at the martial arts school where I used to teach T'ai Chi Ch'uan in South Minneapolis. He knew a lot about Vajrayana, which I was very interested in, and knew a lot about Buddhism, so we struck up a relationship. A short way into it, he started talking about magick, and about Crowley and the OTO, and how he belonged to the OTO. The OTO was Crowley's club. There was definitely a quality of greasiness to the guy, but I've always been attracted to that greasy stuff! Not to get stupid about it, but to acknowledge it, touch it. So it was interesting.

I learned about the Golden Dawn. And I went through the Golden Dawn format—I got the big fat Golden Dawn book. And then there's another great little book by Donald Craig called *Ceremonial Magick,* which was also in the Golden Dawn format, but it wasn't so stiff and Stoic-sounding as that big Golden Dawn book. He had a sense of humor, so I followed his format. I kept a journal every day and I did a tarot reading for myself every day with the Crowley deck and I learned the rituals: I learned the Lesser Banishing Ritual of the Pentagram, and I did the Greater Banishing Ritual, and the Rose Cross and what else—the Middle Pillar—every day. I did that for six or seven or eight months, until I got up to The Watch Tower, where you actually ask for something. You set everything up and you bring in the Archangels, and you are surrounded by all the deities, and then you ask for something. But that rubbed up against my Buddhist attitudes. I thought—the reason we do the work is for the sake of the world and cultivating compassion and Enlightenment—it isn't to get a new car or a girlfriend or whatever—and at the time, the notion of asking for world Enlightenment within the context of ceremonial magic didn't really seem like the thing to do, so I just stopped doing it.

And also, when I did all the banishing rituals, there

was really a very strong feel of armoring: The reason I'm doing the banishing is to armor myself against outside forces or entities. And that wasn't very attractive. That didn't really fit with the T'ai Chi way of embracing and yielding and all that. Though it really helped—in one sense. I broke up with a girlfriend during the time of doing this—not because of it or anything; it was just that circumstances happened that it was appropriate that we break up, but my doing the banishing everyday after we broke up was wonderful, because I was really in love with her and it was a painful event. The banishing ritual really helped.

At the Psychic Institute, I feel, we learned the essence of what all that magic was about. Instead of practicing the Lesser and Greater Ritual of the Pentagram and the Rose Cross and all this stuff, instead of learning all these rituals, you learned the "grounding cord." This involved extending "a cord" from your first chakra to the center of the planet, and *seeing* it there; that is, you would work with an imagined image of yourself in front of yourself on an imagined screen, and you would see this image out on the screen extend the cord. I'll give the instructions on how to do this in a little while. Because it was a "Psychic" Institute, they emphasized your "third eye." It was your third eye that projected this screen and the image of yourself on it, so you were developing grounding from your first chakra and seeing with your third eye at the same time. It is this chakra that runs our *clair-voyance.*

Everything you worked on was on that screen. It's just a pair of glasses. That's what clairvoyance is. A seen event. At the Psychic Institute I would always want to know, "What about feeling?" Their pair of glasses was a visual thing. That's the way they thought about it. Whenever I brought up feeling, they said, "Well you can do both, but don't stop seeing, because that's what we're training."

I discovered then that I am, much more than clairvoyant, *clairsentient.* Clairsentience is a different chakra—it's from the third chakra, your solar plexus. That's a feeling chakra. If somebody walks towards you, you feel them with your third chakra. That's a clairsentient thing. When somebody puts a lock on me, I can feel it. I'm really good at that. So whenever I do a grounding cord, I do it both ways. I see it on my screen, and I feel it too. I give it a little bit of a tug to make sure it's attached to the center of the earth.

❮

The biggest thing that I learned at the Psychic Institute was getting control of the size of my aura, as I described before. At Chen Hsing school we practiced what we called "eight attitude awareness." This was being aware of one's aura in all eight dimensions: front, back, top, bottom, left, right, inside, outside, and then making that awareness big. What do we mean by inside/outside? You might think outside is just the other seven "attitudes." The distinctions get kind of muddy, but what it really meant was this: When I touch something, when I put my hand on something—what am I really feeling? When I put my hand on my couch here, I can say, yeah what I'm feeling is my couch, and there's a texture and it's cold and I'm feeling this spot. Actually, however, what I'm feeling is my hand. So inside/outside is making the distinction between what I'm feeling and the actual *presence* of something. And that's what mind does. You can't get along without getting clear about that distinction.

In fighting, too, you're making that distinction. And it's very paradoxical. For me that's the paradox of the whole of internal martial arts. To feel somebody standing in front of me implies a boundaryless state, and yet to know that this is me and that's them—that implies boundaries. For me to dodge a punch, I've got to feel it, be with it, blend with it, actually feel this person. This is a profound event, and yet I've got to make that distinction between him and me if I'm going to dodge his punch. It's actually out there—this punch that's coming at me.

The essence of this is at the heart of all the Chinese arts, for instance, it's particularly true in acupuncture. On the one hand they stick in the needles and it affects you whether you feel it or not. On the other hand, what they perceive when they palpate your pulses and when they are diagnosing you is something that goes all the way to your own internal experience. It's unlike the way a Western doctor works, which is to locate your body and not be interested in what you feel unless he asks you a specific, usually very limited question. But the Westernization of acupuncture is basically destroying that paradox. They say, for instance, when we talk about meridians or chi, what we're really talking about is bio-energy that's moving through the fascia or the nerves, and so you reduce it back to a purely mechanical situation.

I think that's also the difference between internal martial arts and external martial arts. External martial arts is using that symptomatic approach, saying, well, there's a punch coming at me, I need to use this technique. What this person is feeling and what I'm feeling in relation to him or her isn't given much consideration. Actually, "internal" and "external" aren't so much a way of categorizing the different traditions. Even though people say that Karate is an external martial art and T'ai Chi is an internal martial art, I've met Karate people who are clearly practicing in an internal way and T'ai Chi people who are practicing externally.

I think a practitioner undergoes an evolution from external to internal. It isn't the art, it's the artist. The distinction applies not only to individual martial arts, but to fighting and war-making in a bigger sense. Sadly, that's the way our country is dealing with terrorism—in a completely external way. They hit us, we hit them—the context in which this thing is growing isn't even in consideration.

Another distinction I like to apply is between "Faith-based" people versus "inquiry-based" people. I want to get a bumper sticker that says something like, "Enjoy faith—it's easier than thinking." Faith-based people feel that if they practice, say, a particular T'ai Chi form for twenty years, they'll be all right. They never question or investigate whether they are really growing or learning anything through that form. Their faith stifles inquiry. It's tragic that America in general is taking that path. If you question Christianity and you're a Christian you're a bad guy. Whereas in something like Buddhism, inquiry is encouraged. What is Enlightenment? Is it just an idea? Is it something that we can experience?

Where there's paradox, there is inquiry. Or should be. Internal martial arts is about inquiry all the way through. But for there to be paradox, you have to have two seemingly contradictory things.

The difference between internal and external is very important, and the whole thing is based on the fundamental paradox. Let me try to explain it again. External martial arts tend to be technique-oriented. If a person performs a particular action, like a punch or a kick or whatever, it is met with a particular technique. You learn the technique in an external fashion, but you don't study very much how you have to *be* in order to apply the technique appropriately. The things that give you the possibility of using the correct technique—for doing what has to be done appropriately—that kind of inquiry and training would be more internal. Internal would be more like the listening and the blending and the yielding, and all that demands an internal experience. You have to feel what's going on in relationship; you have to feel what's going on in your body and in your opponent's body. I've got to feel my body, I've got to feel the trajectory of the force and all of that. External martial arts don't train you in that kind of stuff. It's just sort of haphazard. Yes, you learn a technique but it's left up to chance whether you'll intuit how to apply it.

Once again, the internal martial arts are paradoxical. The paradox has to do with boundaries. For me, to feel something, to feel another person, to feel another person's intention or energy implies that I have entered a boundaryless state in relation to that person. To actually feel the presence of another person the way he or she really is is pretty profound. Feeling another person, blending with their movement, may be boundaryless.

And yet, at the very same time, I've got to make a distinction—I'm Ron and that other person is not. If they are throwing a punch, I've got to dodge it. There is a very definite and strict boundary. If there is any confusion about the boundary, then I am going to get hit. So there's both of those things going on at the same time. There's profound intimacy, and yet there's profound separation, distinction. Distinction to the nth degree. And that's a *real* paradox. I've got to feel the line of force this person is intending to manifest somehow, and move out of the way. Or blend with it or accommodate it. It's a wonderful thing.

When I talk to people about this, sometimes they invoke the New Age attitude and they say, "Hey, man, we're all One." I take issue with that. That's only half the story. It's missing the paradox and therefore missing the true wonder. How can we be having a conversation if we're all One? All One? That's what Death is. There's no balance, no two things working off of each other and having a conversation, there's no appreciation. There is no "All One." And yet, energetically, I mean sensation-wise, I am joining with everything through sensation. And so in that respect it *is* All One.

Years ago, I actually had my Christian period! It was when I was in the army, a bit before I read *Be Here Now*—

I had a Jesus experience. I read the Gospel of Matthew, I think it was, during Easter. Something descended on me and I realized it was TRUE. The story of the crucifixion in Matthew is a pretty great story. And for the next three or four months, I was in Grace. I realized that I had been Saved. And I was in Oklahoma, in the army, it was really hot, but the heat didn't bother me, the bugs didn't bite me, and everything was good. I actually felt Saved. When I think back, I've never been happier. But there was a quality of stupidity about it. I didn't have any Will. I didn't have a practice. It was just like something descended upon me, a particular energy was set. Something happened.

In that state I just opened my heart chakra, and poof! It was wonderful. But one day, a Baptist preacher that I happened to be in touch with, called me stupid. I don't remember why, but something happened and he called me stupid. A few days later the Grace went away. The heart chakra closed. And the next thing knew I was reading *The Satanic Bible* by Anton LeVey! And then after that came *Be Here Now*. Which is the thing that stuck.

The Grace thing is still interesting to me. To box well, there has to be a quality of Grace about it. During that original period of Grace—there was no work. It kind of came and went. But now when I was diminishing the volume or size of my aura it was much more conscious. There were people helping me and giving me feedback.

At one point I was talking to the director of the Institute about it. I didn't know how to do it, how to bring the aura in. But then I felt my back, and she said, "Do that again!" And I did it. I *gave* myself permission and it got real easy. But that all had to do with my will. The Path of Will. Because there is a quality of stupidity in Grace—kind of like the Fool in the Tarot, walking off the cliff. With Grace there is no inquiry, no intent.

Though meditation in a Buddhist context may seem to be very passive, actually it requires plenty of intention, plenty of active inquiry. The Buddhist context for training in martial arts always moves me toward inquiry. It moves me toward mindfulness, towards making a distinction between being present and not being present, realizing thoughts as thoughts, knowing when I'm thinking rather than being present in the world. There's nothing wrong with thinking—you've just got to make the distinction. Now I'm absorbed in thought and I'm not "here," and now I'm "here." You just want to make that distinction.

For me, ever since I read *Be Here Now,* Enlightenment has been a thing in my life: What does this mean? What is it? What are the components of it? When I got more into Buddhism, I read a lot about the "mental obscurations" and "emotional afflictions" and the "six realms" that represent different emotional states. It's all really interesting reading, but that's all it is if you don't bring the spirit of inquiry to it and trace it in your everyday life. When an emotional situation arises, you notice: Oh, THIS is an emotional affliction. Like when I'm driving my car and a guy cuts in front of me and I'm starting to yell at him and giving him the finger and I'm not human any more. I find myself in the Hell Realm. Everything is red, all I see is anger, and there are no options, but then POOF: I can change this and say, wait wait—I'm in the Hell Realm and I do have options other than this. That's the mindfulness part. I have a choice.

I've seen some pretty incredible martial artists in my day. I once saw an eighty or ninety year old Ba Gua guy—one of the people trained in China before Mao Tse Tung. What I was mostly interested in (besides his technique, which was what everybody else was there for) was how the guy walked. I noticed how his breathing was, how he was when he bent over to tie his shoe. I noticed his quality of mind. When he walked out the door, I noticed how he opened the door, I noticed how he was in his body, how mindful he was, how awake he was. He wasn't awake just when he was doing martial arts. That's very important to me. Because I've also got this attitude that everything is training. *Everything* is training. If you are living your life unmindfully or are absorbed in thought and not aware of it, or angry or whatever, you're actually training in that: you're gathering momentum behind whatever you are doing. If you choose to be mindful and choose a way that's more human, more compassionate and constructive in society, well, then you are training that, you are gathering momentum behind that. If you are mindful, if you are awake, you can make a choice. Here I am, stupid and angry, it's not helping me, and it has momentum. It's just getting everybody pissed off. But there's a different way to do it. Everything is training that way.

I've mentioned "blending" a few times as part of marital-arts training, but there's a way to apply blending beyond the physical combat or push-hands context. I've hung out with Republican people who love Rush Limbaugh and hunt and shoot guns. I've hung out with them in the garage and drunk cheap beer and talked to them—friendly—there's a way to do it. You don't rub them the wrong way—you act interested. I *am* interested. "Why do you people think the way you do?" Of course the reason that this is hard to do is that you might feel a bit contaminated or compromised. But rather than that, it is possible to actually grow—and feel a little bit bigger.

8

Some Internal Practices

In Chinese medicine our chi comes mainly from three sources. There are more, but I'm talking central generators. We get Grain Chi from the food we eat; we get Breath Chi from the air we breathe; and Ching (Jing) is stored in the kidneys.

Grain Chi is substantially manipulated (enhanced or injured) by the type and quality of the food we eat. Diet includes things like proper mastication, our own physical constitutions, and how they match certain foods, as well as our eating itself. If we are arguing with someone during mealtime it has a negative effect on the digestion of our food and the generation of chi.

At the center of who we are and how we act and respond to circumstances is our breath. How we breathe and the depth of our breath greatly influence how we behave emotionally, psychically, and physically. The lines among mind, energy, and body, lines among emotional, psychic, and physical bodies are very blurry.

Breath chi is enhanced or injured by the quality of our breath—the depth of it, where in our body we breathe. That is, do you breathe primarily in your chest or down in your belly? With a deep inhale the belly expands by the diaphragm pushing your stomach and intestines down and out, allowing more room for your lungs to expand. Chi Kung and other breath work address health and longevity through various breathing patterns, movements, and visualizations.

Simply notice your breath. Notice how you notice it—chest or belly, deep or panting, jagged or smooth, satisfying or not. Once you are paying attention to your breath, notice any accompanying sensation or emotional state. Next time you stress out or are under duress, try moving your attention to your breath.

Put down a grounding cord and get control of your aura. Shoot energy downward consciously. Imagine that link between your first chakra (which is located at the base of the coccyx) and the core of the Earth's gravity. Affirm this link in a way that protects you and allows you to drain negative influences and toxic forces down to the pure-energy planetary core that sends it back where it came from.

In the Asian martial arts, breathing into and storing Chi or energy in the second chakra or Tan-Tien (Chinese) is very important, not only for its calming and centering effect but for power as well.

Your Tan-Tien is located approximately two fingers' width below the navel and inside the body. Breathing into the Tan-Tien, into your center, is also called diaphragm breathing, since it is the diaphragm which expands down, pressing your organs and expanding the belly on an inhale.

Chest breathing is associated with strong emotions, and its accompanying instability can cause inappropriate action. Try ten deep breaths in your chest and see how you feel. Breathing into the Tan-Tien, on the other hand, can be very calming and grounding. It is also a powerful and accessible method of training awareness.

Counting breaths is an easy way to train awareness. Simply count each exhale. Start at one and see if you can get to ten without spacing out or getting lost in a thought. If you do get lost, start over at one. If you make it to ten, start over at one. I often do this as a prelude to my meditation practice, while having my attention on the rising and falling of my abdomen as I breathe (belly breathing). I return to the breath when I notice I've become distracted or more clearly attracted to something else.

Other sources of chi include basic earth energy and that enigmatic stuff called "cosmic energy." The psychic meditation known as "running your energy" that I mentioned earlier and for which I'll give instructions in a minute circulates these energies through your system.

Chakras are localizations or centers of energy in the

human body. I have been assuming that most people are generally familiar with what they are. There are actually many of them—different traditions give different counts—yet seven main ones start at the base of the spine and move up to the top of the head along a central channel—what in the West is called the "Middle Pillar."

The aura is our field of energy surrounding our bodies. Again, I've been assuming that you have some general idea about what this is. It varies in size and quality according to the intent (conscious or unconscious) of the individual.

Having some way to ground ourselves in present-time reality is paramount to living a sane and happy life. Having a grounding cord, doing meditation, running, training in martial arts, in fact, any physical activity, can concentrate and conduct our energy constructively. Besides grounding, having ways to "keep your space," maintaining a boundary, is important. By keeping your space, I mean a couple of things. First we want to keep unwanted influences out of our personal domain and, second, we want to keep ourselves from intruding on others' space.

I'm going to give instructions now for a few simple and pragmatic exercises for keeping your space. Don't worry too much about doing these exercises perfectly correctly. Follow the instructions as best you can. A general rule is *fake it till you make it*. That is, do something that feels more or less like what I am describing until you *really do it*. In the big picture there are no distinctions among mind, energy, and reality, so we have space to play with this stuff. If you fake it for a while, chances are you'll discover internally how to do it for real. Or you may find out that you were already doing it for real and just didn't know it. These exercises are really like games.

This first game takes two people. One person can be A; the other person is B. Okay, now, both A and B: get control of your aura! Ask yourself, How big is it? What's its shape and texture? Can't feel your aura? Fake it till you make it!

A good place to start searching is usually about arm's length from your body on all sides, including top and bottom. This is about where you want it, but in this game do what feels right.

A and B, start out a good distance apart from each other—twenty to thirty feet or so. A, you just stand there and *own* your personal space. B, you own yours as well and, as you do, slowly walk towards A and just notice. Very slowly. Don't lose attention.

A, be aware that, as B approaches, there will come a point when he or she will enter your space. At this point you (A) say, "Stop!" Perceiving aura encroachment involves some sixth sense or awareness of energy not commonly recognized or sanctioned by Big Brother.

Don't worry. Even though you're not Harry Potter or Spock, you've got an antenna for sensing aura boundaries. It's part of your inborn psychic equipment.

Do the exercise again, this time noticing how you do it. B, notice in particular if you know when you enter A's space and how close you come to A's experience.

Now switch roles.

This exercise will teach a lot about how we handle our personal space or aura and how much control we actually have both in keeping others out and staying out of others' space.

This ability is crucial in martial arts. Most great boxers have it, whether they know it or not.

A variation on this game is simply having B or the person advancing be the one to acknowledge entering A's space. Or A, the person just standing, can acknowledge actively entering B's space as B advances.

Do this exercise while maintaining a grounding cord— a rose, a torpedo, or something else. Make stuff up! Play!

I use the phrase "keeping the tubes open" when referring to how we respond to stimulation. For example, if I bang my knee on the corner of a table, I would want to keep open to the sensation, put attention on my knee, and relax. This allows the "blow" to move through and out of my body. If I tighten up, curse, or even curse my own knee for hurting me, I pull my own healing away from my knee and there is a "locking in" of the wound.

A "blow" can be anything—mental or physical. Yes, sticks and stones can break your bones, but names can get into your aura. In the realm of sensation, a blow is pain in the body, anywhere, caused by anything or nothing. There are many ways of addressing it, "keeping the tubes open." One way is the meditation that I've mentioned a couple of times now, called "running your energy" through "microcosmic" and "macrocosmic" orbits.

The microcosmic and macrocosmic orbits are involved in specific Taoist techniques to promote health and long life. These orbits as well as many other orbits, vortices, and channels of chi are "running" in us all the time with high points and low points of "current" throughout the day. These are the foundation of acupuncture.

Two main or central channels bisect the body. One starts at the crown of the head and moves down the front of the body to the perineum located between the genitals and anus. You just feel where you'd least like an acupuncture needle and, yep, that's it. (In fact, it is an acupuncture point.) From the perineum, the other channel goes up the back to the crown of the head, completing the circle. This circle is the microcosmic orbit.

The orbiting of chi or breath can be felt (by clairsentience) or seen (by clairvoyance) or both. Fake it till you make it.

You can start tracking anywhere along the orbit, as long as your attention goes down the front and up the back. Most often, it is better go down the front while inhaling and up the back while exhaling. I've experimented with it the other way too.

The method of inhaling while the orbit moves up the back and exhaling down the front is done also as the orbit moves from the skin and just under it inward to the center of the body. There it is more akin to a single column rather than an orbit. In the Western tradition it is referred to as the "Middle Pillar," as I mentioned.

When you practice this orbit, put the tip of your tongue on the roof of your mouth. Some prefer to use the top of the dome of the hard palate. I try different things at different times, depending on how I feel, so experiment. You'll be breathing in your belly as you do this as well as moving the orbit around with your intention. It may sound like my description implies a gap between your mind and what's happening. There is no gap.

Simply inhale slowly and smoothly while seeing/feeling/intending chi to move down the front of your body. Start either at the crown of your head or at the third eye, or anywhere else on the circuit, it doesn't matter. You just need a point of energy to follow around until it reaches your perineum where you exhale, moving it up the sacrum into and up the spine to either the crown of your head or your third eye, depending on where you started. You can do it as many times as you want. Just make sure you do it with attention and intention.

▶

Now let's run some energy.

This is a meditation I learned at the Psychic Institute. Sit comfortably in a chair with both feet flat on the ground and your back comfortably straight, and with your hands resting palms up on your thighs. The emphasis is on clairvoyance, the center of which is the sixth chakra located in the center of the head at the pineal gland. This chakra is also associated with the "Third Eye," between and above your eyebrows. Close your eyes (for now). Put your attention in the center of your head. To find it touch your Third Eye. With your other hand, touch the back of your head on the opposite side. Draw an imaginary line between the two points. This will trace the center of your head from front to back. Now touch the left side of your head at the same height as your Third Eye with one hand, and, with the other hand, touch the opposite side. Again, draw an imaginary line between the two points. Where all four lines intersect is the center of your head, your clairvoyant center.

Now imagine or "see" a screen about two feet in front of you. This is where you will project an image of yourself sitting in your chair. The choice of seeing yourself from the front, back, or side is up to you.

The next thing you want to do is create a grounding

cord. This is to be a connection between you first chakra (your "survival" chakra), and the center of the planet. Remember, the grounding cord can be anything you want it to be: a beam of light, a waterfall, a tree, a rose, whatever. Just see it on your screen. The grounding cord's function is to redirect any energies, thoughts, sensations, feelings, beings, people, voices, pictures, etc., you don't want in your space. Just let it all run down your grounding cord (have a big, strong cord!) to the center of the planet where it will return to where it came from—no damage done.

Now we want to bring up earth energy through the chakras at the soles of our feet, so, from the center of your head projected on your screen, see earth energy from deep in the planet seep and run into your feet chakras. Let it run up through your calves, through your knees and thighs, picking up any unwholesome energies along the way to your first chakra, where it goes down your grounding cord to the center of the planet. Give your brand of earth energy a nice earthy color suitable to you.

Next you want to bring in cosmic energy. From the center of your head, see cosmic energy from way out there in the universe among the galaxies coming to you. Don't go out to get it; it will come to you. It meets your body at the top rear of your head where the two channels start moving down on either side of your spine. This cosmic energy touches and spins through all the chakras on the way down, cleaning them out. Then it continues down to the first chakra where it blends with the earth energy and goes down your grounding cord. Give it a nice "cosmic" color suitable to you.

Here at the first chakra is where energies mix—say 40% earth energy and 60% cosmic energy. This union of flows goes down your grounding cord to the center of the planet, cleaning and fortifying it on the way down. Now the remaining 40% earth energy and 60% cosmic energy: move it from your first chakra up the two channels on the front of your body, guiding it up towards the top of your head, touching and cleaning the chakras on its way. Keep your grounding cord throughout.

At the crown of your head the mixture of earth and cosmic energies blossoms up and out like a fountain reaching its height and cascading down on all sides. This fountain of energy defines your aura. At a point just beneath you, you can tuck it in to your grounding cord like a shirt into a pair of pants. This fountain also cascades from the tops of your shoulders down your arms making little mini-fountains coming out your palms.

The last part of this meditation is called, "The Gold Sun." On your screen from the center of your head you want to create a big gold sun over your head. This is your own healing energy; it is a major power magnet. It brings back your own energy from wherever you left it—maybe with your parents, or with an old lover, or at school, at work, perhaps at a friend's house. Be creative.

Consider. Where did you really leave it? Where were you sloppy? Where do you forfeit your center, your sense of your own cosmic ground, your worth?

This energy is yours and will come to your Gold Sun. You don't need to go out and get it. Let it fill your Gold Sun; allow it to get bigger; warm it up. When you feel it's ready, open the top of your head and let it flow into you, filling every cell of your body. Do it as many times as you need to, until you fill yourself with the (your) gold energy.

9

Martial Arts as I Teach It

Boxing (I use the word in a large sense, to refer to any spontaneous sparring, grappling situation) demands a degree of presence unneeded in normal daily life. For example, if you are walking on the rocky edge of a cliff, you're probably more attentive to your body and physical surroundings than, say, at the office or at the store. Boxing demands attention as does walking on the edge of a cliff. If you "go away," for example, if you leave your body, i.e., if you psychically space out, you fall from the cliff or get hit. In both examples you would experience consequences for not being present with your awareness.

Our typical urban environment doesn't demand our presence to the degree that, say, rock-climbing, skateboarding, or skiing do. Of course, there are moments, like crossing the street or driving, that demand our awareness, but it's still typically the out-of-the-body variety of awareness. Boxing involves much deeper internal awareness; otherwise, all your skills are overwhelmed by the confusion and energy of the situation.

My martial-arts teaching is based on some really basic precepts:

Unless you train yourself in violent situations, how you'll act if you find yourself in one will be no more than a guess.

See advantage in disaster. A punch towards my head is either an opportunity or something disastrous.

The more control I have over the situation, the less damage I have to do.

The more control I have over my internal experience, the less damage I will do to others and myself.

With all the crazy shit happening out in the world, what each of us has 100% control over is how we're going to act— retaliation or revenge or something else.

It's the people closest to you who have the potential to hurt you most. My double meaning here is intentional.

Peter Ralston says:

> It is the freedom, power, and clarity attained by the warrior when he has truly adopted the state in which he, as an individual, is already dead. 'As if already dead' was the warrior's life and power. This is not seen in a morbid or a noble sense. It is as a complete and total surrender (sacrifice) of the self-identity, the individual, the illusion of an independent self. Only

when this is so is there no more tendency to be distracted by, trapped in, or confused with any particular form. However, this must be so every moment. It must be so beyond time. It is the same as surrendering to the truth and giving up your self-demand. It completely undermines the tendencies that arise from the survival and protection of the self-identity.

Tui Shou or "push hands" is the foundation of the Chinese-originated martial art of T'ai Chi Ch'uan. In the game of push hands, two people each try to find their partner's center or substantiality and uproot it or project their partner into the air.

In the realm of martial arts, when facing an "opponent," we want to be open to seeing what they see, to seeing what they want. Since "combat" (from push hands to all-out fighting) is the game here, we want to feel/see what our partner has targeted so we can lead their actions with that target. In fact we can choose their target by simply offering them a target. We do this by creating the situation whereby their going for what we offer is the easiest and most efficient thing for them to do. They don't even consider anything else. In order to do this we have to feel ourselves as the target and to offer ourselves, getting our opponent to focus on what we offer. And if our opponent chooses a target other than what is offered, we have to be open to seeing/feeling that change and then lead with what they have chosen.

Leading is the natural extension of what in T'ai Chi Ch'uan is called "yielding." Yielding is simply what it says, yielding to an incoming force rather than blocking or struggling against it. Yielding is the natural extension of blending with an opponent in a momentum and mind. Blending is "attaching" ourselves to our partner's movement. There is no interference here; we simply move with our partner—same trajectory, same speed. To do this we have to deeply and correctly interpret our partner's action and our relationship to him or her. Interpreting is the natural extension of listening, which is being open to and aware of what is going on, moment by moment.

It should be obvious that in order to cultivate these internal skills we need to sincerely acknowledge our own internal state. This includes our mental and emotional layers as well as what is perceived directly through our senses: sight, sound, smell, and touch.

We need to be precise. This precision includes our opponent whom we need to acknowledge. That acknowledgement will give us the opportunity to choose how we will respond to any situation, including violence.

If we are mindful of our immediate environment and sensitive to the actions and attitudes of the people around us, we can often nip any tendencies toward violence before anything violent happens. After having been very competitive and aggressive myself, I am very sensitive to that energy in others, and that knowledge gives me the option of de-escalating the situation. Yet if I were unaware and hooked into matching that energy, things could escalate and bad feelings would result.

▲

I don't think people want to be intrusive or rude unless they're assholes, and even then, underneath an asshole's behavior, is fear and pain. Even appropriate violence used in self-defense or in the defense of others has fear at its base. Having an attitude of protection, "of being on guard," has fear at its foundation. If we can make a distinction between their behavior and them, we can create some space in which we act appropriately rather than react to our own impulse towards violence—whether it's a violent or retaliatory act or simply the thought of it.

I remember a discussion I had with my brother Rob at a restaurant where we went to eat. When we found the place too busy to be immediately seated, we went to the bar to wait for a table. As we sat down my brother remarked that it was interesting that, after so many years, he would still check out everyone (men) in the room. Who could he beat up, who would give him a hard time? I told him that I used to do the same thing and on occasion still do and that this protectionist "stance" had a corresponding energy or "feel" to it. This is related to the way we trained at the Cheng Hsin school. Peter Ralston had us train in "eight attitude awareness," as I mentioned before. Eight-attitude awareness, if you remember, is being aware of what's in front of us, behind, to the right, left, above, below, as well as what is our internal state and what is external or in the environment. Then we trained to be very big with it—to fill up a room with our eight-attitude awareness and to practice engulfing energy. I also told him how often this checking is fear-based.

One of the things I found attractive about the Psychic Institute was that they talked about *matching* energy. If you get into a room with, say, military types, there's an energy about the situation that's set—set military energy. And you'd be hard-pressed not to match it. We tend to attune ourselves over time to whatever we're hanging around. So at the Psychic Institute, they talk about how you can set your energy consciously, intentionally. For instance, you can set your energy on "party," or set your energy on "compassion" before you walk into a situation. It's your choice. To set your energy before you go somewhere, you visualize the situation and, simply, set the energy! There isn't much more to it. If I'm going to give a demonstration of some martial art, I can set the energy for confrontation and violence, so that I can get challenged and beat some people up and make a name for myself as a hard-assed martial artist, or I can set the energy for learning, realization, and a demonstration of the grace of the practice.

▶

The ability to fight with grace and effortless power has mindfulness as its foundation—mindfulness of self, or our experience, of whatever is in our field or awareness, including the body, thoughts, and emotions of ourselves and of the other person, as well as of the physical environment. That's a lot to be aware of and can be overwhelming. That's why we have safeguards and boundaries: to keep from being overwhelmed. As our practice of mindfulness deepens, our sense of groundedness deepens as well.

We want to ground ourselves in our bodies and in the planet, the literal ground that we stand on. We want to feel the pressure of our gravity in our feet and legs, as well as having awareness below us, actually in the ground. We want to use that pressure to manifest "chin" (pronounced "jin") which is effortless power.

Skills or powers in boxing include listening, interpreting, and leading. These are internal events. That is, they are not dependent upon a particular body posture, technique, or stance. The cultivation of these skills is saturated with the cultivation of mindfulness. I can neither listen, interpret, lead, nor manifest chin if my attention is elsewhere.

It takes study and practice to be able to hold so much in our awareness, to be able to be present in body awareness—being grounded, relaxing, using the whole body, paying attention to what's going on, dodging punches, neutralizing pushes, and still listening to what someone is saying.

The study of internal martial arts is learning how to get bigger, how to hold more sensation, more awareness, without freaking out or going stupid, but actually staying mindful and relaxed.

I once saw a nature show about bears on TV. There was this giant grizzly looking kind of inquisitive but also a bit nasty. The narrator said something like, "You really want to be careful with this guy because he doesn't have the capacity to sustain a lot of ambiguity." Well, that's okay if you're a grizzly; in fact that's your only choice. But as a human being, you have to sustain a lot of ambiguity *and* paradox to be a good fighter. You have to be simultaneously in your own and your opponent's mind. A bear isn't going to pursue that. In fact, when his tolerance for ambiguity runs out, he's going to make his choice.

To begin developing mindfulness, feel your hands. I've chosen to begin with hands because of their familiarity and our almost constant use of them. So . . . just feel them.

Feel that they are there and they exist. Feel that the sensation of them doesn't stop—that is, until we put our attention elsewhere.

When I say "feel," I don't necessarily mean touching your hands one to the other. I simply mean, feel them whether or not they are touching anything.

If you close your eyes, how do you know you have hands?

In fact, how do you know you have a body?

Notice if your hands are conceptual or tactile. Your body likewise. Do you just *think* you have hands or do you actually feel them?

With your eyes closed, notice the depth and quality of sensation. How much of your hands do you feel?

Slowly open your eyes and notice if this has any effect on your experience of your hands. Do this several times, each time trying to keep the depth of your experience as you open your eyes.

Just sit with your hands for several minutes and notice when you start thinking about something else and what this does to your experience of your hands. Maybe your experience of your hands is replaced by your thinking as if your hands no longer exist.

This style of meditation is the practice of "returning." In this case the returning is to the sensation of your hands. Feel your hands and, as soon as you're aware you're not feeling them, return.

From our hands we can start to include more of our bodies until we fill ourselves with awareness.

▲

It is very difficult to live our lives this way. We have to think. Thinking is not bad. We just want to recognize thinking as thinking and sensation as sensation. This is the foundation of meditation/mindfulness, of being awake.

Getting clear on the relationship between thoughts and reality is at the core of mindfulness practice.

It's also true you can't be a successful martial artist unless you can make this distinction. It is very subtle. You need to make the distinction between what you think is happening and what is in fact happening. I can think a punch is being thrown and react as if that's what's happening, when in fact there is no punch. If I do, I am vulnerable to getting hit because I'm hypnotized by my thoughts.

The only difference between meditation and internal martial arts is that in martial arts you can get hit, while in meditation you return to your sensation, whether of your hands or of breathing. But getting hit is just a way of reminding you to return to sensation. Unless you're encountering deadly force, it's no big deal. In fact, it's an aid. In some meditation schools, the teacher whacks the students doing zazen (sitting on their cushions) with a stick to keep them alert to sensation.

After a while I "got it" that martial arts is meditation and the way to not getting hit was to return to my sensation of myself. Once I was back in my own body, I could feel and also see what was going on and I could dodge a punch. Whenever I became disengaged from the relationship by spacing out, leaving my body, I'd get hit. T'ai Chi boxing is a very dynamic meditation practice.

This knowledge is no more than interesting conversation unless we embody these principles. There are a lot of people out there who would do very well on a written test. Tibetan Buddhist teacher Namkhai Norbu, while giving advice on the presence of awareness in his book *The Mirror,* makes a distinction between sustained Presence and Awareness. He tells a story about a cup of poison. The normal adult would not only not drink it, but would warn others not to drink, since to imbibe would cause death. On the other hand, someone who knows the liquid in the cup is poison yet lacks continuous presence might therefore allow his or her attention to drift; the unfortunate result might be that he accidentally drinks the poison.

The point is that if awareness is not accompanied by sustained presence, it is difficult to produce the right results. You can *know,* but you have to be present in that knowledge. The options are only two: you have sustained awareness; or you are in a state of unconsciousness, spaced out and on autopilot with nobody home. Then you are lost in the momentum of "the robot," the blind movement of the force of Karma.

Remember: I can teach you how to meditate, how to box, how to get some distance from your thoughts, but if you spend the rest of your time, the remaining 164 hours a week, doing something else, being pissed off at how things are, it's not going to work.

Do you ever *truly* realize that there's as much space behind you as in front of you? Do you ever feel your back?

Don't get hypnotized by the drama. Stay sober. The goal isn't activity. The goal is awareness. You want to die awake, to realize your last breath as your last breath. The world will be saved one mind at a time. You are 100% responsible for yours.